THE HEALING ART

The Desire to Heal

The Other Man Was Me

What the Body Told

Diva

Landscape with Human Figure

The Healing Art

A DOCTOR'S BLACK BAG

OF POETRY

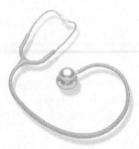

Rafael Campo

W. W. NORTON & COMPANY

NEW YORK • LONDON

Since the copyright page cannot legibly accommodate all the copyright
notices, pages 207–9 constitute an extension of the copyright page.

For information about permission to reproduce selections from
this book, write to Permissions, W. W. Norton & Company, Inc.,
500 Fifth Avenue, New York, NY 10110

Manufacturing by The Maple-Vail Book Manufacturing Group
Book design by Chris Welch
Production manager: Anna Oler

Library of Congress Cataloging-in-Publication Data
Campo, Rafael.
The healing art : a doctor's black bag of poetry / Rafael Campo.—1st ed.
p.cm.
Includes bibliographical references.
ISBN 0-393-05727-5
1. Campo, Rafael, 2. Poets, American—20th century—Biography.
3. Physicians—United States—Biography. 4. Physician and patient—
United States. 5. Poetry—Therapeutic use. I. Title.
PS3553.A4883Z466 2003
811'.54—dc21   2003006677

W. W. Norton & Company, Inc., 500 Fifth Avenue, New York, N.Y. 10110
www.wwnorton.com

W. W. Norton & Company Ltd., Castle House, 75/76 Wells Street,
London W1T 3QT

1 2 3 4 5 6 7 8 9 0

for the poets, whose words sustain,
and, as ever, for Jorge—physician-scientist,
my love, my heart-and-brain

Oh, to vex me, contraries meet in one:
Inconstancy unnaturally hath begot
A constant habit; that when I would not
I change in vows, and in devotion.
As humorous is my contrition
As my profane love, and as soon forgot:
As riddlingly distempered, cold and hot,
As praying, as mute; as infinite, as none.

—JOHN DONNE, FROM *THE HOLY SONNETS*

ACKNOWLEDGMENTS

I am grateful to Brandeis University for the opportunity to serve as Fanny Hurst Endowment Visiting Poet, which afforded me the time to develop the lectures for my "Literature and Healing" seminar that served as the basis of this book.

I am also indebted to Dr. Thomas Delbanco, former chief of the Division of General Internal Medicine and Primary Care at Beth Israel Deaconess Medical Center in Boston and professor of medicine at Harvard Medical School, whose humane example not only inspired this work but also encouraged its completion.

My editor Alane Mason provided me with invaluable guidance during the creation of this book, and I am thankful for her great faith in me as a writer and her even greater kindness to me as a friend.

I can never repay the generosity of David Baker, Olga Broumas, Mary Baine Campbell, David and Kathy Coen, John Dugdale, Robert Pinsky, Kim Vaeth, and John Vincent, whose thoughtful and enthusiastic responses to the ideas raised in this book spurred me to more rigorously define them.

Acknowledgments

I thank Peter Zusi, lecturer on Slavic languages and literature at Harvard University, for his helpful and insightful comments on my discussion of Miroslav Holub's poem "Suffering." Finally, to the patients and their families whose stories contributed immensely to the realization of this work, I give you every tribute that my own words contained herein can humbly carry.

CONTENTS

Contents

THE HEALING ART

"Daniel"

Nearly every day, I find myself thinking about a patient of mine, who I will call Daniel. Soft-spoken and shy, Daniel has struggled with depression for as long as I have known him; his symptoms have long been resistant to a variety of antidepressant medications, and to numerous pro-longed courses of psychotherapy. I will never forget when, just over a year ago, he tried to commit suicide; later that week when he came in to see me for follow-up, the harsh winter sun-light intensified to what seemed like divine truth by the reflec-tive metal blinds of my clinic office, his bright blue eyes welled up with tears as he produced a sheaf of papers from his knap-sack, folded neatly in half, which he told me would explain why. "Us poets are supposed to do these kinds of things," he said with a forced smile and a clumsy swipe at his eyes with his wrist. A warm teardrop fell on the back of my hand as I reached out into the storm of full-fledged sobs he couldn't stifle; another marked, as it ran across them, the pages he handed to me.

Reading what he gave me later that night, I learned for the

first time, in poems that seemed crafted to contain in each one a small, precise detail of what had happened, that he had been a victim of sexual abuse by a parish priest in the town where he grew up, a sleepy community somewhere just east of the Berkshires. At once an expression of his pain and the unwillingness for fear and shame to talk about it, these poems, as it turned out, became a crucial catalyst to his recovery. Daniel recently moved away from Boston to the Southwest, happy in a new relationship, full of joy in the responses he has received to a literary webzine he designs and edits, and still writing the poems that help to keep his dark moods at bay.

When I think of Daniel, I try to resist the temptation to let his story become a facile metaphor for the power of language—and of poetry in particular, with its signature capacity for speaking the unspeakable—to promote healing. Surely his depression and its lifting are more complex than that, a myriad of intersecting influences and predispositions, some biological, some pharmacological, some cultural, some spiritual; just as surely, it cannot all be entirely resolved with the stroke of a pen, and he must still feel rage, or degradation, or confusion and fright when he relives what happened to him. Yet there is something undeniably important about the role of words, of narrative and poetry, in the process he underwent, something utterly courageous and humane in his handing those poems to me, the awful and yet irrepressible document of his suffering. More than important, really—his poetry seems in retrospect like a prerequisite, fundamental condition to his healing, because without it, his abuse experience almost surely would have remained unaccounted for, unmarked, as though it had never happened, leaving only his intractable symptoms in its place. I felt joined to him in his words, in the act of his writing, the two of us united in the interplay of writer and reader, of speaker and listener, of sinner and confessor, of small boy and authority figure, of victim and witness, of human being and human being, implicated in his plight in these and countless other ways that my Harvard-approved medical training had never allowed me to envision—and that several years of competent, standard medical care had failed to uncover.

How well I knew the data of his disease! I had skillfully elicited his symptoms of insomnia, anhedonia, inattention, and poor appetite, I had accurately characterized the neurovegetative signs he manifested in our interviews, and I knew which medications had been tried and for how long, and what the limiting side effects had been. Blood analyses had ruled out anemia, HIV infection, and hypothyroidism as possible underlying causes of his profound listlessness. But it was not until I shuddered at the cold hands of the priest closing around my own throat, and registered the helpless shame as I felt my dungarees being jerked down—rendered indelibly in the compressed and rhythmic language of his poetry—did I begin to apprehend what had gone so horribly wrong with Daniel. It was only then that I could begin to intervene more effectively, to meet his revelations with some hard thinking of my own.

I well know that I am not the first to ponder the relationship between language and healing. Theorists in quiet, well-appointed libraries have ruminated abstractly on their connection—and have reached fascinating conclusions. Yet when I sat down to write this book, what filled my heart seemed a more pressing obligation, an urgent call to action. I wanted to focus attention on what I have always regarded more as a highly charged fusion than an interesting intellectual question. My motivation was palpably acute, like the adrenaline surge I feel as a doctor rushing into a chaotic emergency room. I wanted to create a place where some of the poems I so love and often employ in my clinical practice—great and necessary poems that perform the harrowing and joyful truths about illness—could be experienced, center stage, in the same way I became subsumed in Daniel's life-affirming, status-critical poems. I wanted to redress what I felt was almost a kind of neglect, one that has as much to do with the panic and terror that so harmed and haunted Daniel as with the worsening failures of a model of medical practice driven by merciless financial bottom lines to the brink of disaster. I imagined poetry might, if given the chance, even heal medicine itself. By presenting actual living-and-breathing poems and my responses to them—and in some cases, responses that have come from my patients as well—I hoped to create an irrefutable argument for preserving compassion and nurturing empathy in medical practice, and by extension, perhaps, in society at large. The poems I chose to discuss were written by people who do not enjoy the luxuries and comforts of the academy or the corporate boardroom to shield them from the body's truths; they are dying of cancer, they are kept from sleep by pain, they are despondent to the point of swallowing an overdose of pills. They spend hours staring into the glaring lights of the ER, wondering what will happen to them next, trying to seek comfort in the sound of their own hearts beating. And yet they have devoted some of their precious and dwindling energies to making poems.

So I think of Daniel, perhaps at his own desk now, perhaps with a view of windswept Arizona desert out the window that seems to him a stark depiction of how he once felt: a desolate and unforgiving landscape in which survival seemed impossible. I imagine that he begins to write, as I do now, beginning to see the faint roses and golds and greens in the endless sands and hunkering mountains, the graceful pose of a cactus, the stunning, unrelenting blue of the cloudless sky—the rapturous beauty all around in what once might have seemed so hopelessly barren. Perhaps he tries to imagine the incantations of Native American people, whose spirits inhabit the land; he must also want to tell a story, just as I do, just as they did, to create a representation, to make some sense out of what once seemed incomprehensible. Perhaps he connects the faint song of sparrows rolling in his yard's dust to clean themselves with the remembered sounds, just as near and innocent and cheering, of a church choir rehearsing. Is it a kind of call to prayer, the dim echo of a passage from Isaiah? When he writes down what they say to him, what we can share, together, is not just the poem but also the possibility of healing.

I

INTRODUCTION

"Clara"

One of my former students, for whom Clara seems an appropriate pseudonym, once warned me of the limitations of trying to link poetry and medicine. An intensely smart septuagenarian whose dark eyes darted and glittered under a shock of closely cropped white hair, she had cared for her husband as his own once lively mind disintegrated from Alzheimer's disease, nursing him even as she faced her own diagnosis of endometrial cancer, and then the discovery on self-exam of a breast lump. (In her commanding, no-nonsense presence, more often than not I had felt as though I was *her* student—as when she had matter-of-factly confided in me all this personal data in the process of asking my permission to audit a class I was teaching at Brandeis University.) It was a late night seminar I had called "Literature and Healing"; I would drive the twenty-five minutes there from the hospital each week with a mixture of exhaustion and exhilaration, as if the distance between my two vocations were as easily traversed as the little-trafficked shortcut I had discovered. It was not too long into the semester, after one of our class meetings, that she first took me to task. It was only October, but the week's twenty-degree temperatures already felt like winter. The tall oak trees had been completely denuded the night before by a freak windstorm, their acorns and leaves scattered around as though the whole campus had been ransacked—as if in the frantic search for truth, or at least the minimum knowledge required to pass midterms, I thought wryly to myself. All was just barely visible, beneath a full moon so clear and white it gleamed like polar ice. "Rafael," she called out to me firmly. We paused inside the intimate cone of light carved from the frigid dark by a streetlamp on the path back to my office. Our conversation became curling and rising shapes as our breath turned to steam.

The class had just finished reading Susan Sontag's *Illness as Metaphor* and *AIDS and Its Metaphors*, in which the well-known novelist and literary philosopher expresses her dismay at how many of our disease metaphors stigmatize the afflicted. In particular, she elucidates how those with cancer, mental illness, and AIDS are harmed by our, and their, imagining their suffering as self-inflicted, or even deservedly punitive, the result of either repressed feelings or (and the opposition itself is instructive) licentious behavior. Perverse and not always so expansive or generous, our very human imagination, she suggests, can kill. Anecdotally, I could think of many patients in my own practice of medicine whose cases poignantly bear out some of her conclusions: the middle-aged woman newly diagnosed with breast cancer who blamed herself for never having left her unhappy marriage, another reproaching herself for her lifelong weakness for butterfat; the nose-pierced recipient of a positive HIV test result who lamented that he brought it on himself for not being more careful in choosing his sexual partners, or for simply being gay; and the heroin user who just last week had told me he knew he was "asking for it" by not toughing it out back in detox. By resisting the timeworn metaphors of "disease = self-defeat," Sontag insists, we may foster a healthier way of being ill.

My students were also reading *Illness and Culture in the Post-modern Age* by social anthropologist David Morris, examining how the specific problems of the postmodern condition, as he defines it, further complicate our relationship to the disquieted body. His version of postmodernism, in which culture and biology are equal in their power to shape human lives, offers some relief from the scientific model of medicine that came to prominence in the age of modernism. Morris believes that strict reliance on hard science oversimplifies the illness experience; he sees the rise of technology as cold, and woefully insufficient for deliverance of the "sick soul" imagined by the likes of Pound, Moore, Stein, and Eliot. Here, too, abundant examples from my own clinical practice flooded my mind: the elderly Costa Rican immigrant on anticoagulation therapy for a prosthetic heart valve whose worsening obtundation due to a slowly accumulating subdural hematoma was repeatedly misinterpreted by nurses and house officers in her chart (under the heading of "Neurological Examination") as "Patient unable to speak English"; the African-American woman whose chronic back pain was exacerbated by miscalculated epidural injections performed by anesthesiologists who then quickly labeled her a drug addict and therefore refused to prescribe narcotics to her; the young couple undergoing infertility treatments who told me their reproductive endocrinologist said their questions were a sign of anxiety that would only make it that much harder for them to conceive. If only we depended less exclusively on biomedical science, Morris seems to say, and instead gave more credit to information readable only in the ill's subjective experiences as *expressed by them,* perhaps we could improve their care, prolonging more lives and alleviating more suffering.

So a kind of impasse presented itself as we imagined the journey to the country of the ill—the inescapable country Sontag envisions in which, she pointedly reminds us, we all eventually hold "a more onerous citizenship," the same destination which in Morris's view is frankly ubiquitous in our tabloid-crazed world of Marlboro-smoking cowboys plastered on billboards and well-hyped celebrity battles against bulimia or sexual addiction. I reflected on these two conceptions of illness during my short weekly commute, on ill-lit side streets that seemed to become more and more winding; an unwitting experiment for my own class, I couldn't help fretting whether my sleep deprivation was going to catch up with me someday, and wondering if the grande double espresso I craved really might keep me going indefinitely. Not only are we inundated in bromidic metaphors that can give rise to shame or guilt or despair when some dread diagnosis is reached; at the same time, the reductive and divisive ways in which the illness is actually arrived at, diagnosed, and treated today, and then exploited by our omnivorous media outlets and seized upon as the territory of one specialized commercial, scientific, medical, or academic discipline, only further tears us from ourselves. The students, including Clara, were deeply troubled: it seemed we were all doomed to be left stranded, comfortless in the throes of our collectively flawed thinking, at the inevitable moment of our greatest need, with neither alternative engendering much in the way of healing.

One wonders, then: How much does what we imagine about illness really impact on our prospects for getting well? Might I really cut short my life or magnify my own anguish by obsessing about unhygienic sleep patterns or spending too much money in pursuit of an illusion created by Starbucks? Clearly Sontag's and Morris's lines of thinking are in important ways at odds with each other, though each seeks a fundamentally truthful understanding of illness in our moment that might encourage recuperation. My aim in the class (as in this book) was not to dispute either of these authors' arguments, nor to align myself with one or the other, but rather to continue, and perhaps to enlarge, the discussion they have initiated. And, most centrally, to inject into it at least one hopeful rejoinder to the invidious forces they describe—poetry, of all things—by which the ill can yet imagine (and have long imagined) healing.

Clara's nagging concerns about all this were really twofold: on the one hand, she was resistant to any approach to the remaining materials on my syllabus that would be too antiseptically academic, and at the same time she did not believe that the more subjective readings, especially the poems, would adequately capture all the muddy diversity of possible responses to illness. (I had guessed at her incipient frustration by the frown she wore as we debated the virtues of the two authors in the vacuum of the classroom ringed by much younger, wrinkleless, and otherwise unmarked faces.) She was still seething with anger at the loss of the intelligent, gracious man she had long considered her soul mate, particularly at what she considered the indignity of his death, and her own sense of degradation at being forced to bathe him, to spoon lukewarm oatmeal into his mouth, and to choose for him what clothes he would wear each day. She was equally skeptical of any theory that might hold that simply writing about an ordeal such as hers could be healing, and mistrusted any poem that proposed or enacted such a transformational process. She did not feel especially illuminated or transformed by what she had gone through. She felt just plain tired from lying in bed sleepless with worry about whether her children would meet her husband's same fate; her bones still ached from all the times she had tried to lift him from the commode; and she was scared about the results of her imminent mammogram.

I responded to Clara by explaining that I did not intend to provide any definitive answers; I said I understood how her own experiences of illness had fomented painful questions in her that might not have any answers at all, but maybe the texts could provide a new kind of opening into this difficult realm. Even for the most theoretically oriented writers, their own illnesses were a starting point where they had to leave previous assumptions behind in order to embark on their writing projects: Morris alludes to his chronic back pain, and Sontag even more bluntly refers to her own cancer diagnosis and the bleak prognosis she went on, as she wrote her essays, to defy. I told Clara I expected she might feel even more angered, or vexed, or even frankly dispirited by the works she would go on to encounter in the class, but that it seemed to me that taking this risk was worth it. She might be surprised, or at least challenged, to see what she had suffered in a different light—perhaps even to reconsider it all, to reinhabit it. To enter into this field of investigation was an opportunity for her to contribute her own timbre and chord to what I have always considered a kind of chorus of voices, one that is not necessarily well rehearsed or even harmonious, and to hear how the sounds of sense might thus be altered. She would be allowing the texts into her consciousness on mutually negotiated terms; illness would not be foisted on her, unbidden, again.

"Hmmm," she said as the wind began to rise again in the narrow courtyard, causing the bare trees above us to sway slightly, like nimble fencers preparing for another round of swordplay. I could see her mulling over some of these possibilities. I imagined a new narrative taking shape in her mind.

A half-smile surfacing at last, she seemed at least partly persuaded by my arguments, and then gripped my arm tightly as we headed to the warmer but otherwise not much more hospitable domain of the gray concrete block known as the graduate studies building. Months later, after a successful seminar throughout which she consistently offered some of the most startling and instructive insights, she wrote to me to say that she is now writing her own story about the grief she experienced at the intersection of her husband's dementia and her endometrial cancer—and celebrating the news that the breast biopsy done after her "suspicious" mammogram result revealed only benign glandular tissue.

The way we regard illness, as Clara's wariness makes plain, is not by any means static or "one size fits all." Hers is a kind of practical working definition, one that asserts illness is neither distillable into a pure theoretical concern nor merely the thorny subject of a work of art. It follows quite obviously, then, that neither can our responses to illness be unidimensional, whether here in this book, in the groves of academe, in the glaring ICU, or anyplace else in our lives. We must affirm that illness, even as we externalize in theory and in art, even as we seek to pin it down so we may rid ourselves of it through medicine, is essentially and undeniably part of us; it is the blood irretrievably lost from the open wound, it is the awful urinal we must empty, it is the brittle skeleton showing through a malnourished body. Once acknowledged as both dynamic and deeply internal, evanescent and yet ingrained, it seems we can proceed more honestly, eyes wide open, and thus much more productively.

Just as our notions about Sontag's examples of the ancient scourges of tuberculosis and syphilis have changed radically— from romantically fatal to eminently curable—so too do our ideas about today's major diseases. From mad cow disease to the Ebola virus, to hormonally induced cancers and now even to the possibility of bioterrorism, we can see deflections in thinking that are driven as much by science as by how we imagine science, and as much by evolution itself as by how we understand that process, too. "Old" diseases can even become new again, as case rates of tuberculosis and syphilis are on the rise in our major urban centers, fueled by the greater closeness between people made possible by increasing access to such diverse technologies as air travel, antiretroviral "cocktails," and Internet chat rooms—and despite competing advances like broad-spectrum antibiotics that could eradicate these infections. My alcoholic patient in twenty-first-century America is the hapless, innocent victim of a "new" disease, declared by the latest science to be caused by a genetic deficiency in the way her liver metabolizes the large volumes of ethanol she consumes. Two centuries ago in this same nation, she would have been condemned as a moral failure and a blight on her community, in need of strict spiritual rehabilitation, perhaps even confinement. Millennia ago, in the times of the Druids, amidst her mysterious ancestors across the Atlantic, she might have been considered a powerful seer whose drunken ravings were fearsome and privileged communications from the gods.

Amidst such shifts and revisions, Morris does well to call our attention to the specific ways in which postmodern society further shapes the experience of illness, fragmenting it into distinct, discordant realities (instead of emphasizing the vulnerability we all share). He points out, for example, that not just the subjective experience but even the actual quality of health care provided for the same illness in America today is measurably worse if you are black than if you are white—the subjective crossing inopportunely into the quantifiable. Globally, on an even more appalling scale, such disparities are all the more painfully evident: over ten million deaths from AIDS are expected in sub-Saharan Africa, while the affluent industrialized West has at long last begun to see a decline in AIDS death rates in certain of its subpopulations. Just as dismaying, the pesky case of traveler's diarrhea I nonchalantly treat with a course of Cipro in my patient back from Nigeria on banking business is also the terrifying disease dysentery that kills many thousands of Nigerian infants and children each year with no access to such medication, never mind clean drinking water.

Much more could be said of scholarly discourse in this area that debates the relative power of scientific fact versus human possibility in effecting responses to illness—whether Sontag's brand of fiery intellectual polemic or Morris's more inviting postmodernism-made-easy (not to mention the writings of many others who have made their own valuable contributions). No matter how clearly we grasp it, perhaps more than anything for our purposes here, its richness and complexity can be taken as an expression of the significance of this nexus. It is important—indeed, critically so—for each of us, future patients all, to examine the link between the healing and the imagination, to reawaken the bond between body and soul, to explore this territory not merely as some wasted battleground on which science and culture duel but as a living garden of what the humane mind might be able to accomplish. For even the most ambitious theories come and go; great ideas are proposed, then are retracted or rethought or disproved, leaving us with the painfully material truths of such slippery entities as alcoholism and AIDS. What remains ineffably constant, it appears, across all illnesses and cultures and throughout all of our known history as a species, are two quite simple human facts: not only do we suffer—the unsentimental admission of which was Clara's sine qua non—but also, just as fervently, we must make sense of the experience of suffering. In other words, we must tell the story of what hurts, *all* of its stories, just as sensible Clara seemed to have so promptly concluded. (Or, to paraphrase Nancy Mairs, who calls herself "a homely writer," trained both by a Ph.D. program and her far more grueling education by multiple sclerosis: affliction perfects human experience, as only her own kind of limpid eloquence so well demonstrates. Her graceful crossing of disciplines helps make apparent that academic hypothesizing, and even technological invention, is really just another adaptation of storytelling, neither more nor less valuable than so-called creative writing—poetry, fiction, memoir—that theoreticians sometimes look down upon, but which will be the foundation of the rest of this book.)

IF SONTAG'S ARGUMENTS are marred by too exacting a desire to strip *all* metaphor away from the experience of illness, delivering cancer and AIDS and depression out of our messy cultural fascinations and distortions and into the coolly dispassionate, "objective" hands of modern capital-S science, so too does Morris fall short of an alternative approach that truly honors the myriad particular narratives of illness while at the same time making full use of the universalizing power of empathy.

Science, as has been proved over and over again, is never as objective as it is supposed to be, and has often produced more harm than good when enlisted to solve the innumerable problems of human affliction; one need only look back at Nazi medical research that supported the warped theories of eugenics and racial superiority, born of modern scientific methodologies, to see its frightening inadequacies. (Even the vainglorious notion of "solving the problem of human affliction" ought to warn us of the limitations of science at its most arrogant, perhaps too ready to boil us down to mere quantities for its equations; suffering is no mere computation to be figured out, but a defining condition of our humanness.) While, on the other hand, elaborate postmodern theorizing takes place in a world of deepening human conflict that it has yet failed to revolutionize, many would argue that fellowship is only imperiled by its ascendance. Perhaps we have become too enamored of the fragmentary and the individual, as our stakes in ever more narrowly defined identities grow—we are smokers or feminists or Nuyoricans or born-again or "cat people" before we are Americans, or even more fundamentally, human—and we militantly defend these categories, leading to polarization of ideas and what seems a burgeoning (if unintended) intolerance of "the other." What medium, then, is left that can accommodate the daunting task of addressing human suffering in our time? Is there any form of human expression, any reliable construct of our imagination, that can handle the telling of a story so difficult and multifaceted, and yet so essential?

Poetry. Individual poems like those I shared with Clara and

the other students in my class, poems like those I often offer to my patients. Metaphors are the stuff of language's magical limitlessness; empathy can yet transcend postmodern "differences." When charged with new metaphors that conceive of illness in life-affirming, literally heart-thumping language, poems are that impossible yet universal expression of our basic human selves. At the same time, poems are lightning bolts of idiosyncrasy that illuminate empathy in their afterglow; they have the amazing capacity to hold many (even at times fractious) narratives in their thrall. Poetry at once takes us back to our origins as a species—before the invention of text, rhythm, and rhyme surely facilitated the oral transmission of stories encoded with essential information from generation to generation, and helped knit together our earliest communities, contributing to humankind's survival. Yet to this day, poetry remains an innovative, living art form that in each new iteration reinvents itself. In poetry, the instinctual and the emotional coexist on a par with the intellectual and the rational; poetry disallows the separation of these realms, which are so often and so wrongly considered to be at odds with one another. Poems can at once make us feel sorrow and help us to understand a new concept. And through the poem, the weighty impact of emotion on our thought processes—one neurologists are only beginning to map—can be more clearly parsed.

We might even consider the impulse to produce poetry as biologically determined, hardwired in the way even the most rigorous of technicians would appreciate, and thus *necessary* for our survival. As Morris tells us, we seem driven to create narratives, and he cites a host of provocative psychological studies to prove his point. We fabricate stories with the same kind of visceral compulsion that drives us to explore our environments or to fashion tools. Poem-making, then, is akin to arachnophobia, or sexual attraction, something we cannot help but manifest. Poetry is in our blood, is as shared among us as the 99.9 percent of our genetic material that makes us all members of the human family. Surely it is a universal experience to be struck by the beauty of a quiet, snow-covered vista, or moved by the intense colors in a sunrise, and then to feel almost immediately the urge to recount it, to jot down some fleeting impression, to record and thus preserve that uncanny sense of what we have witnessed as emblematic of a deeper truth. Such inspiration, and the reflexive desire to pass on the wisdom adduced to others, is the source of all that we know as poetry.

In fact, poetry exists in almost every human culture, and poems read to us in languages we do not even know can still arouse responses in us. We can be calmed by the sonorous rhymes in thirteenth-century Italian of Dante, and enchanted by the pleasing, almost danceable rhythms in a ghazal written by a contemporary Kashmiri poet we may never have heard of. Poetry in the form of pulsing hip-hop lyrics connect urban African-American teenagers and millions of their counterparts in predominantly white suburbs across the United States and in other western European nations; poetry in the form of prayer and hymn links many more millions within their faiths, and sometimes (too rarely) across them, all over the globe. Given poetry's unique location at the intersection of the physically embodied and the cul-

turally imagined, no other medium seems as well suited to con-
sider—or to encompass—the illness experience: whether to
revise the cultural fantasies and misapprehensions Sontag cri-
tiques (fueled as much by bogus or misinterpreted or overblown
science as by superstition), or to enliven the novel "biocultural"
model of illness Morris proposes (defined not nearly so specifi-
cally by other prose forms of narrative).

A particularly salient problem for any so-called biocultural
approach to healing, even one informed and enriched by
poetry, nonetheless remains: what to do when culture itself
becomes supersaturated with the solutes of science and technol-
ogy—when poetry itself gets technologized? Increasing num-
bers of Americans nowadays have come to expect a little pink
pill to relieve them of stress, a painless laser procedure to
improve their vision, or an odorless topical cream to rid them of
cellulite; most doctors, rather than delving into the time-
consuming complexities of the psychosocial realm, are more
than happy to oblige with a quick fix. We are all too easily
seduced by anything that is newfangled, pioneering, and avant-
garde, especially if it might help us lose weight, preserve our
youthful appearance, or live longer. Mouthpieces for the Human
Genome Project grandiloquently describe the code of nucleic
acids it is unraveling as "poetic"; in fact, it is rather monotonous.
(Even the beauty inherent in the double-helical structure of
DNA, famously described by Watson and Crick in what some
have elevated to a "prose poem" published in the journal *Science*,
seems a bit exaggerated in the splashy light of unmitigated sci-
entific progress.) Meanwhile, the old masters' paintings are sub-

jected to X rays and chemical treatments in the effort to expli-
cate precisely how they were created. These days, even poetry
itself may be at risk of this kind of appropriation, becoming a
dominion of specialists involved in a brand of writing dubbed
"experimental" that only the most rarefied of literary critics can
comprehend (not unlike, one might say with exasperation, cer-
tain whistles that can be heard only by dogs).

It seems that such deliberately antiempathetic poems might
only further alienate us from ourselves, frustrating narrative and
sacrificing emotion to the exercise of deconstructing syntax and
exploding language. "*Poetry,*" I have heard some of my patients
groan, suspiciously or with distress, when I first introduce this
approach to them, their verbal italics an expression of the kind
of mistrust that some such poets and literary critics have them-
selves bred. Quiet panic too often ensues when the subject of
poetry comes up in polite conversation; too many of us have
been inculcated with the false notion that poetry is intelligible
only to an elite few, even though it is all around us, not just in
the lines of Shakespeare we never forgot from college or the
passage from Auden that adorns a popular movie but in the lul-
labies sung to our children and the psalms read in Bible study
groups. That contemporary poetry is inaccessible or even irrele-
vant is one of the most common complaints of its detractors
among the brave general readers who do still frequent their
independent bookseller's shelves. Yet they are responding to the
snobby efforts only of a few. Of course, the irony here is that
"inaccessible" work, and our recoiling from it, only tends to
reaffirm our dependence upon, and pleasure in, the sense-giving

power of language. Perhaps this lesson is the purpose of experimental poetry writing, to demonstrate by its deprivation that which we need to console us, to comfort us, to illuminate us.

More ominously, perhaps such poetry aims instead to hyperextend the possibilities of human communication, reflecting back to us our love affair with instant messaging and cell phones and DSL—a kind of harbinger of a time when we will accept technology so completely that we will welcome it even into our own bodies, in the form of genetically engineered organs or bionic limbs. Maybe by then what we think of as culture will have been wholly replaced by the Orwellian nightmare of pre-programmed, passionless ideology ("Click here to download what to think about . . .")—or worse, language will be successfully disjoined from its primary purpose of conveying sense. Yet in the meantime, despite these looming concerns, poetry remains the most stalwart of all the belles lettres in its devotion to the profound connections between mind, body, and soul; indeed, if poetry and medicine can be reconciled in the ways I hope this book will show, then perhaps we can begin to mend more meaningfully the larger antagonism between the humanities and the sciences that since the modernist collision of science with the arts has interfered with genuinely productive collaborations. Perhaps we can make what was once called "the art of medicine" seem not merely quaint but respectable, even indubitably honorable, again.

The writers with illness whose work I shall contemplate have made poems that are first and foremost *accessible* in the way truly great poetry must be. For the most part, all were born during the past century, and are considered by their peers and their readers (and even some critics!) to be among our most important English-language poets. (The prominence of these writers itself seems to signal the importance of a poetic means of examining illness.) Though many eminent poets have written about illness—how could they not, since infirmity lies at the intersection of so many of poetry's vital themes?—I have chosen to study individual poets who have devoted a substantial portion of their lives' work to the experience of illness. Many continue to create art today that they view as necessary to their survival. What they repress, or leave out, has as little to do with how they became ill as what they express, or spill out onto the page. (I will focus in this book on the work of poets, but of course other forms of creative self-expression, ranging from visual art to music to sculpture, may also embody healing.) The more important concerns for these artists, and perhaps the most appropriate and relevant questions to ask of them, is how they have become transformed by their suffering, and how their creative self-expression has in turn defined their illnesses.

My strangely hybridized work as a modern-day physician-poet—a rare breed if ever there was one, a questionable and shifty species, perhaps overbroad in its thinking—no doubt colors my readings of these poems. I offer them not as authoritative abstracts but rather as possible interpretations that can coexist among the many that my readers are sure to feel as deeply in their own hearts. I intend them as suggested, well-marked paths through the poems; along the way, I fully expect other readers may notice salient details and important relationships that have escaped my eye, and which may outshine or conflict with my observations and understanding. Even the arrangement of the poems here is open to question—many of the poems I have selected might have been deployed in one or another section of this book, and many other poems by the same poets, and by others who have also explored the experience of illness, might have been enlisted in this discussion. I welcome such diversity of opinion; the poetry itself invites it. May any disagreements lead to more attentive and wider readings of these poems, and others.

Especially exciting to explore here is just how poetry locates us *inside* the experience of illness, demanding that we consider it from within as attentively as we do from without. These poems, whatever we might decide they mean, will undoubtedly make us feel tightness in our chests, or make our ears burn; they will clutch at us like death's icy hands. They will also restore us after a long day, possess us to read them aloud in bed to our lovers. They will mold our facial expressions, widening our eyes and instigating our smiles, and they will even alter the sound of our own voices as we declaim them while shampooing in the shower. In some cases, they literally live on after their authors' demise; surely all of them will outlast not just the poets who made them but each of us, too. I think of these poems as a means of entering into the minds and bodies of the ill, just as they so readily take hold of me; their effect is akin to placing one's ear against the patient's heaving chest instead of listening through a stethoscope, or touching an enlarged lymph node with one's warm fingertips instead of coolly perusing a biopsy report.

In presenting specific poems for discussion, I have made a conscious decision to maintain each offering's textual wholeness. Though dissecting my cadaver in medical school may have helped me to better understand the fine points of anatomy, I also remember how the exposed vascular networks and delicate neural webs and isolated organs, even as I appreciated their glistening beauty, became less and less a whole human being beneath my scalpel's sharp blade. In a similar way, chopping up the poems into their constituent stanzas and lines feels too invasive, too disruptive of their intricate workings, even if to do so might make for easier study. I felt that a more holistic approach was required here, one that treated each poem as the quirky, conflicted, long-winded, difficult, musical, and demanding entity the poet conceived, even if it meant making my own narrative less fluid. Doctors are notorious for speaking over our patients, preempting their narratives with torrents of medicalese, interrupting even their answers to our own questions with our appropriated, preconceived version of what is happening to them. If only symbolically, I wanted to let the poems have all the space and time they needed here, to luxuriate across the page in the way patients may not in their narrow hospital beds with restraints and side rails, to demonstrate once and for all the respect they (and the poets who made them) deserve.

In choosing to focus my energies largely on poetry that has been published by prominent poets, poems that have already borne the scrutiny of a public audience, I have also made the implicit decision to protect the privacy of my own patients, whose writing, whether published or not, may often contain information about their health or other personal data that they would not wish to disclose in this kind of forum. In the few cases where I have felt compelled to draw on my patients' poetry and narratives, I have been careful to change names and to alter details to ensure that their specific identities remain confidential; whenever possible, I have also asked for permission to include their narratives in this book. In the cases of those who refused to grant such permission, I am reminded to note here that writing about illness need not engage its audience on the literal page of a magazine or book, in the raucous domain of the public record, as another of poetry's key characteristics is its immateriality. Thus poems can be memorized for one's own private benefit, secret talismans that might be invoked to ward off panic attacks while traveling on the subway—or even to be meditatively recited aloud while doing yoga naked in the living room, with no one to hear but one's pet goldfish.

While it may very well be another kind of hubris for a physician-poet to assert that poetry in any of its guises can cure breast cancer or bipolar illness, what these writers have to say does get essentially at the more complex and mystifying process of healing. That is, curing and healing are not the same, and it is possible to achieve the latter without succeeding in the former. By taking up that challenge of the poem, these poets are no longer at the mercy of our society's misguided attempts to make sense of their illnesses by imputing to them our own hobbling fears and unarticulated rage. With each handwritten, sweated-for line, they refuse to have our postmodernly inflated and academically glitzy categories of race, sexuality, and ethnicity imposed upon them. At times they may fiercely contradict the biomedical narrative of their illnesses, while elsewhere they may gladly and collaboratively welcome it. Even if they may at times respond to these external pressures, or even articulate them—indeed, we must expect them as poets to speak at once metaphorically and idiosyncratically!—I contend that they do so surely not to satisfy any of our theories, but instead to ameliorate very real symptoms.

The poems under discussion, then taken, together, suggest a larger formulation of, or movement through, the experience of illness—one that interrogates the overly reductive postmodern model, and at the same time reforms the argumentative, rigidly science-driven biomedical discourse postmodernist thinking alone cannot derail—without resorting to the hysterical or the unreal. The ulterior narrative of disease these humane poems flesh out is seamless and supple, integrated as symphonically as the body itself. It begins intuitively, even before symptoms appear, and then takes us through the familiar stations of symptoms, diagnosis, treatment, and its inevitable side effects, and at last, for some, to cure and recovery—or for others, no less healed, to the end of life and beyond, into transcendence.

Fully aware of all that is ultimately unknowable about how we suffer and die—from my vantage point at the precipice of the hospital bedside, where even the most sensitive and accurate measurements of physiology (however appreciatively and beautifully described by all the Nulands and Sackses of this world) cannot assuage—I provide these readings and analyses not as complete explications of the power of this work, but rather as an invitation to consider and to feel the full scope of that power, which must consist at least in part of the uniquely human capacity for empathy. Our neglected but never relinquished empathic aspiration, our mightiest common dream, arises not from the practice of medicine, nor of literary criticism or philosophy, but only from great poetry.

II

Language and Healing
in History

Various forms of structured language, and especially
what we recognize as poetry, have been important
and even principal means of healing throughout his-
tory and in many different cultures, even after the advent of a
more sophisticated understanding of the human body's anatomy
and pathophysiology. During the modern era, poetry flourished
in an important sense as a *response* to the alienation and fear
engendered by once inconceivable scientific advancement.
("Make it new, make it real!" was the battle cry as poets like
William Carlos Williams, himself a physician, sought to reinvent
a more genuinely democratic, organic, New World idiom for
their craft.) If any mode of human expression can be said to
have an almost universal affiliation with illness, as many before
me have attested, it is poetry.

Incantation and poetry were the primary means of healing in
Native American cultures for many millennia. Cabeza de Vaca, a
sixteenth-century Spanish explorer, provided the first detailed
written record of the healing practices of indigenous people in

his *Relación*, published in Spain in 1557. He himself adopted the techniques of the Capoque Indians, who inhabited for about two thousand years the Gulf Coast of present-day Texas; he describes, in language notable for its lyricism, how he grew to be highly esteemed among them by curing abdominal pain and puncture wounds, and even reviving the dead by blowing breath into the afflicted person's mouth and praying over the body, thereby casting out the illness. The Navajo "night chant," a centuries-old poem passed down orally through countless generations, integrates the human body into the larger natural world and addresses the spiritual implications of physical illness. Calling upon the stars, the moon, the sky, the sun, the corn, and the land, all in the context of the sufferer's community, it relies for its therapeutic effect upon the belief in what literary scholars have termed "the magical instrumentality of the voice." The Iroquois "condolence ritual" made use of similar tenets of Native American belief systems; its ceremonial incantation led by a medicine man or shaman dealt specifically with grieving and depression in the wake of the loss of a loved one. These and many other Native American traditions of healing employed performative language, and understood healing in the holistic sense, applying not just to the physical but also to the emotional, spiritual, and communal realms. Many compelling accounts exist of dramatic cures effected by these practices.

The Egyptians of the pharaonic age expressed their belief in the connection between language and healing by giving their dead a book, a kind of guidebook to the afterlife, without which survival of the spirit was unimaginable. The Book of the

Dead, as it is known, was inscribed with charms and spells to serve various purposes in the hereafter. It also contains beautiful hymns in honor of the great gods Ra and Osiris. Though little is known about its use in the ancient burial ritual itself, it is clear that this advanced civilization believed that a written text was necessary to guide the deceased in their perilous journey to eternal life by helping them to overcome the various tests and obstacles on their way.

The ancient Greeks, whose highly evolved culture perhaps more than any other forms the foundation of our own, also believed poetry and healing to be inextricably interrelated. The crucial importance of this relationship was unmistakably represented in their theology. Apollo, the most revered and awesome deity in the Greek pantheon, was god of both poetry and healing; among his symbols were the lyre (the harplike instrument whose music often accompanied the declaiming of poetry) and the staff, which retains to this day its identification with medicine. Apollo's son Aesculapius was the god associated with physicians and was believed to have invented the art of medicine; the Muses, the seven goddesses responsible for inspiring poets, musicians, and artists in their crafts, were his daughters. The shrine of Aesculapius at the ancient site of Epiduarus, said to be among the most beautiful in all of Greece, demonstrates in its physical construction the inseparability of poetry and medicine: the *abaton,* where supplicants slept in anticipation of a cure, which would come to them in the form of a dream, was immediately adjacent to the *tholos,* or theater, where the great dramatic poems of Greek culture were performed. According to Aristotle, the catharsis, or emotional turning point in these tragedies, was often linked either to physical healing or to physical affliction, and delivered an intentional and expected effect upon the audience.

Much in the Judeo-Christian tradition also joins poetic utterance and healing. Biblical poetry such as that in Psalms and the Song of Solomon makes frequent reference to the physical body and contains many prayers for the healing of conditions as varied as depression and infertility. Some of these traditions continue to have expression in the current day, where, for example, faith healing thrives in many revivalist and fundamentalist churches across our country, or in the formal teachings of Christian Scientists, who rely strictly upon prayer for the treatment of illness. Christ himself, who some theologians and scholars believe bears a distinct resemblance to the Greeks' Apollo, is often shown in the Bible to have healed with only words; most dramatically, he revives Lazarus with the simple, divinely iambic pronouncement: "Come forth!" Gerard Manley Hopkins, an important religious poet of the 1800s, repeatedly imagines Christ as both a poet and a healer, and Christ acts often as a powerful muse not only for him but also for many other devotional poets.

During the Middle Ages, the body itself was "read" or interpreted as a text, and manuscripts meditatively produced by monks contained such "prescriptions" as exhortations against the sinfulness that was thought to cause disease, and specifically linked prayers for healing. After the revolutionary development of the printing press, and as medicine concomitantly evolved into more of a rigorous science—and as scientific disciplines in general began to lay greater claim to the human imagination— the relationship between words and healing changed but did not disappear. Books only began to be used more formally in medical contexts. By the 1700s in Europe, for example, reading was often prescribed as "moral treatment for the insane," as one physician of the time wrote, updating the medieval practice. Books went on to become perhaps the most important antidote to the dehumanizing effects of the Industrial Revolution, which with its new technologies ushered in both centralized hospitals and terrible new diseases. Even the renowned visionary physician Benjamin Rush, in planning his Pennsylvania Hospital of 1810, established a library so that inpatients could read up on subjects prescribed by their physicians. (Rush's Pennsylvania Hospital, most will recall, is considered the precursor of the modern American "medical center," like the one I work in today.)

This practice of prescribing literature to patients as a form of therapy continues today in what is called bibliotherapy. In a recent review of bibliotherapy that appeared in the *Canadian Journal of Psychiatry*, Katz and Watt define modern bibliotherapy as "the guided use of reading, usually as an adjunct to psychotherapy in mental health care settings, for learning about and developing insights into illness, and for stimulating catharsis, to aid in the healing process." These authors describe a number of conditions in the treatment of which bibliotherapy has proved successful, from social phobias to depression. (Least surprising of these, perhaps, is sexual dysfunction, which supports the age-old romantic belief that poetry is especially effective in wooing and inspiring potential lovers.) There even exists in the literature a report of a randomized controlled trial of bibliotherapy in chronic schizophrenic patients which purports to show that chronic schizophrenics who were randomly assigned thrice-weekly reading sessions which included poetry exhibited fewer behavioral problems than those who received the usual care. While the author does not explain in detail the nature of the improvement in patient attitudes, the results are intriguing nonetheless, particularly in light of some of the long-standing theories regarding the therapeutic effect of psychoanalysis. Among analysts, one school of thought holds that the efficacy of psychotherapy lies in its ability to provide critical structure— something like poetic form, one might say—to disturbed thought processes, thereby helping to develop the insight and sense of reality so useful to the mentally ill patient.

Other scientific work has begun to investigate the effect of poetry more directly on basic human physiology. With data published in the *International Journal of Cardiology*, German researchers have shown that metrical poetry, when read aloud for thirty minutes, slowed their subjects' pulse rates, as compared to those who engaged in normal conversation for the same period of time. They hypothesize a "harmonic interaction" between heart rate and respiratory rate, perhaps mediated through neural connections between the language centers in the cerebral cortex and the lower brain structures that govern autonomic nervous system responses, that tends to synchronize these cardiopulmonary functions; as a consequence, blood pressure may drop, allowing tense muscles to relax. Such "proof" only bears out what any of us knows from the familiar experiences of singing hymns in church or calling out cheers at baseball games or chanting slogans at political rallies or meditating in stress management classes: rhythmic language helps us breathe more deeply, makes our hearts pound more steadily, and reminds us that our heads are joined to ecstatic, flesh-and-blood bodies.

An indirect therapeutic benefit of poetry can be imagined in the impact it can have as an instructive tool upon aspiring physicians (and other care providers). Surely the flourishing interest in medical education circles over the last decade in the "medical humanities" is a renaissance that bodes well for the future of medicine. August medical journals such as *The Lancet* and *Annals of Internal Medicine* have begun to publish poetry by physicians and people living with illness; one can find medicine and literature courses springing up in the curricula of medical schools across the country. More and more care providers are following in the footsteps of such literary luminaries as Anton Chekhov, Walt Whitman, and William Carlos Williams; several literary journals specialize in publishing doctor-writers, and there is even a weekly E-zine that circulates physician-poets' work on the Internet. Anecdotally, from my experience of meeting medical students and residents, and their mentors who are beginning to teach humanistic materials alongside of cardiac electrophysiology and renal tubular acidosis, it appears that a resurgent movement is indeed afoot—one that harkens back to the mentoring that once was at the heart of the apprenticeship of an aspiring physician, and which may someday reclaim medicine as the art it truly remains.

Perhaps more immediately relevant to general medical practice, just within the last few years another randomized controlled trial appeared in the prestigious *Journal of the American Medical Association* that showed—and the significance of these findings cannot be overstated—that among patients with chronic and debilitating medical conditions such as asthma and rheumatoid arthritis, those who wrote creatively about their illness experiences reported fewer symptoms and exhibited less disability than those receiving usual care alone. This result is shocking not solely because modern-day physicians actually thought to investigate a hypothesis as humane as one that posited a relationship between creative self-expression and healing but also because the "emotional" or "subjective" (usually so stridently dismissed as impossible to quantify) was quantifiable in these terms. Not just calming the pulse rate, or providing reassuring insight into what it might mean to be sick, but modifying the course of disease: the act of writing here seems to heal, as the relentless deterioration caused by two very different and yet equally complex illnesses was stalled with nothing more than paper and pen, language and imagination. So vaunted is the biomedical understanding of illness today that patients themselves often demand tests or diagnostic procedures to explain their symptoms, and then the medication or surgery they presume will cure them; the allure of technology itself seems to motivate them as much as the articles they read in health magazines or on the Internet that rightly empower them to take charge of their health. It is inspiring to see amidst such pressures that the subjects of this study remained open to the possibility of the healing power of their own narratives, a low-tech way to be "proactive" that might afford even greater benefits.

Such research begs further questions, one perhaps most acutely: Why might poetry be therapeutic? Though the breadth of historical examples of the marriage between poetry and healing is intriguing, and the continued successful use of literature in psychiatric and some medical settings is suggestive, precious little "scientific data" exists to support its effectiveness. As David Morris notes, mysterious phenomena such as the placebo effect, which he defines as "the power of belief to initiate physiological processes," have been demonstrated in countless similar studies and yet remain largely ignored, or taken for granted, or scoffed at; less familiar, equally disregarded data, generated by a prominent physicist at Princeton University and also cited by Morris, contends that human consciousness can influence otherwise randomly mechanized sequences of information from an isolated, tamperproof machine. Even prayer, which undoubtedly shares its roots with poetry, even in this nation of diminishing secularism, is viewed with skepticism despite preliminary clinical studies that show its therapeutic effectiveness.

After all, one might be tempted also to ask the usual variation of this question, one that has been kicked about in many quintessentially postmodern settings of late, from highbrow literary magazines to community college departments of creative writing): What use is poetry at all these days? Is it even remotely possible that any study, carried out by epidemiologist or poet, could be devised that might accurately gauge the indispensability of the poem? For the answers to these questions, let us pull ourselves away (if we can) from validating science, and open our minds to the music of the poets themselves.

I I I

"*Sunny*"

S unny, as I will call her, is a slight person, in her early sixties
now, Korean by birth but raised here in the United States,
in Pennsylvania, where her parents immigrated when she
was just an infant. Her face, round and crinkly and faintly ruddy,
reminds me of the huge pink peonies she once surprised me with,
cut fresh from her garden last summer. When we first met, Sunny
was contending with what another physician had diagnosed long
ago as fibromylagia; later she underwent a skin biopsy for a mole
that appeared atypical to me and which proved to be a melanoma.
As I sometimes do with new patients, I slipped a few photocopied
pages of verse in among the oddly cheery patient education pam-
phlets ("From Fatigue to Fantastic!" "Q and A: Chronic Myofas-
cial Pain," "The ABCD's of Self-screening for Melanoma"), some
relevant scientific articles from medical journals, and the usual pre-
scriptions. For many patients the poems are a springboard to a
refreshing reconsideration of their health concerns; they are fre-
quently the first thing they want to talk about when they return
for follow-up. But Sunny never acknowledged them.

An artist by vocation, Sunny had given up painting during her youth to raise her family, but in recent years she has returned to it, with evident pleasure. I suspect she is lonely, since her children are scattered across the country and her husband is dead, so at the very least I imagine her painting fills her days with something to do. Her fibromyalgia, which causes stiff joints and severe muscle aches requiring narcotic analgesics for control, has seemed to improve the more time she spends at her canvases; whether her relief is due to the stretching of her limbs that her technique requires, or from the expression of her pain in the abstract, almost tortured images she produces, is ultimately irrelevant. What remains most important is that she feels better when she paints, less exhausted from her poor sleep; I've thought, especially after seeing how she makes use of art in the face of her illnesses, that poetry would appeal to her even more than to most of the people who come to me for care. I don't want to give up, not yet.

But Sunny, despite her moniker, is what most doctors would categorize as a "difficult" patient. Our most recent visit seems a typical one. When I call her name, I am as always running late; Sunny signals her frustration by a long glance at her watch and with a deep sigh before she slowly rises and makes her way into my exam room. The waiting room, that cramped theater of suffering and dread, provides a sympathetic audience. An elderly African-American woman in a wheelchair starts to babble incoherently, as if distressed by my rudeness, while a smartly dressed younger version of her holds her hand tightly. A young woman in mismatched tank top and sweatpants, obviously thrown on at the last minute in the effort to drag herself in, erupts into a fit of coughing that tosses her long blond hair into her face. "Always so busy," I hear my next patient mutter to her daughter under her breath in Spanish, with just a hint of disapproval. Already an unspoken narrative of disorderly human feeling is taking place, which is at odds with the one I immediately begin to impose by reaching out to shake Sunny's small hand, mechanically, with firm professional authority.

It takes Sunny a few minutes more to settle into a chair once I've closed the door behind us. She is clad in navy blue slacks, their polyester material stretched smoothly over the lower part of her protuberant belly, and she clutches her black purse so tightly it seems she fears I might snatch it away from her. Her T-shirt is ablaze with the huge yellow head of Tweety Bird, wearing an exaggerated frown and proclaiming something in a bold-faced caption that is almost entirely hidden under her belt line. Her tan orthopedic shoes have flecks of paint on them, which I notice as she takes another minute or two to align her feet precisely beside one another under the chair. Finally, she stares straight ahead, concentrating on what I assume is her utter misery. The small exam room offers her little alternative, I suppose; windowless, with the wall-mounted sphygmomanometer dangling its cuff like some awful miniature gallows, its most attractive feature is the Matisse art print that hangs almost impudently above the exam table, with its simple arching black figure displaying its tiny ember-red heart.

Almost immediately the telephone rings with the practice assistant asking whether I will still see my 8:10 patient, who has arrived an hour late and says he is dizzy. A clock inescapably occupies the wall directly above and behind Sunny, timing her as it does all the diabetes and urinary incontinence and insomnia in the world. I need to know Sunny's pain score and how she is managing her ADLs—on a scale of one to ten, how bad have her wrists been, is she having trouble with shopping or housecleaning. I know that fibromyalgia is a chronic condition whose ravages occur over decades and pervade all aspects of its victims' lives; more than the isolated fatigue, or pain, or insomnia it causes, it seems to lay waste to that almost inexpressible sense of well-being that the rest of us take for granted. I know my brusque interrogation is unfair, impossible to counter meaningfully even if we had hours of time at our disposal. Still, she obliges with answers, in broken English, that as we rush through them sound more and more rote, as hollow as my close-ended questions. I don't press her, though, as I am already negotiating with myself about how little I need to do of the physical exam; after all, her complaints are all too familiarly unremitting, so what new information will my fingers' poking and prodding yield? Sunny continues to stare impassively before her, oblivious, or perhaps even willfully unmoved, by my evident distress.

I suddenly find myself glaring at her, trying to contain my anger, which finally rises to the surface of my consciousness, bursting past the barriers of professionalism and emotional anesthesia that I built up during my medical training. My free-flowing rage seems a response to everything from managed care to unchecked immigration, from the inadequacies of my biomedical knowledge to address conditions like fibromyalgia to

the culture of a nation that devalues its elders. I seethe in the
Gordian knot of a cruel, irrational question: Why should I have
to take care of this horrible old woman whose own family has
abandoned her, who ought to be torturing some doctor in
Korea anyway, whose lousy insurance won't even reimburse me
for my time, whose behavior seems perennially antagonistic, and
who won't get better no matter what I prescribe since she has a
disease that many doctors do not believe is real at all?

Though I am no invincible general of antiquity, I realize I am
at the threshold of a useful metaphor. Poetry could be the
gleaming sword that cuts through this knot; better yet, since my
conquering, destructive impulse is already beginning to fade, I
can conceive of language as an instrument by which I might
more gently loosen and perhaps even untie it. I look at Sunny
again, her round peony face, her inexpensive, sensible, stained
shoes, her gleaming black leatherette purse. I ask if I can help
her up onto the exam table; she pulls back at first, then looks at
me for the first time during the visit. After a few moments, she
gives me a small half-smile and holds out her arm for me to
take. I ask, "Did you ever look at those poems I gave you?"
Silence. I am thinking she might like something by David
Baker, whose stunning collection *Changeable Thunder* I've just
read. I am remembering some lines from a poem that deals with
his struggle with chronic fatigue: "How to combat exhaus-
tion?/I can see that the other//exhausted, tears off/a fragment
of this fatigue//in order to give it to me./But what am I to
do//with this bundle of fatigue/set down before me?//What
does this gift mean?/'Leave me alone?'//'Take care of me?'/No

one answers, for what//is given is precisely/'what does not answer.' "

"Would you like to look at some poetry together, Sunny?" She moans a little, wincing with the effort of standing. Time seems to ease its grip on us; the exigent world stops its screaming.

"Maybe," she says.

IV

Inklings

W hen does illness begin?
Arguably, diseases start with certain environmental exposures and human behaviors that are believed to cause or to predispose to them. Epidemiology shows us that smoking leads frequently to lung cancer, injection drug use with shared needles to hepatitis, high-fat diets to coronary artery disease and obesity, unprotected sexual intercourse with multiple partners to HIV infection. Thus we should be able to prevent disease by controlling or eliminating our risk factors—a beguiling notion, at once potentially empowering and yet perversely pernicious. The possibilities for assigning blame to the ill abound, while seductive science becomes the final arbiter of our every action. Inconveniently, the distinction between promoting salubrious choices and decrying "vices" easily blurs as we are faced with ever-multiplying, often contradictory scientific studies. Such ultimately inconclusive data prompts us to ask: Can a fondness for chocolate really be equated with a heart attack? Is consuming too much fat, or too many carbohydrates, what will

eventually do us in? Our actions as individuals and as a society must certainly impact on health, but are individual passions any more unhealthy than the sedentary lifestyle fostered by the great advance of the automobile, diets thrown out of balance by wealth or poverty, or freethinking characters turned fatalistic by the belief that our vaguely defined "genetics" are omnipotent? Surely out of this murkiness, and yet before any frank symptoms are manifest, an intuition, a sense of something gone awry, has prompted many a worried telephone call to the doctor to schedule that long-overdue physical. In this mysterious realm of the portent, the nagging malaise, the unspoken unsettlement, poetry begins to delineate the terrain of illness. It is here, at the very source of the disturbance, into which all our astonishing technologies fail to probe accurately enough, that poetry first gleans the immensity of what lies ahead. The act of poem-making creates meaning from uncertainty, converts foreboding to knowledge; it is a way of entering the body, another form of ultrasound (literally) that produces far clearer and more detailed and nuanced pictures of the internal landscape. So perhaps now is the most apropos time to introduce the first poem.

The Tree Warden

I. A FAREWELL TO ELMS

In late July, now, leaves begin to fall:
A wintry skittering on the summer road,

Beside which grass, still needing to be mowed,
Gives rise to Turk's-caps, whose green tapering ball-
Point pens all suddenly write red. Last year,
The oriole swung his nest from the high fan
Vault of our tallest elm. Now a tree man
Tacks quarantine upon its trunk. I hear

An orange note a long way off, and thin
On our hill rain the ochre leaves. The white
Age of a weathered shingle stripes the bark.
Now surgeons sweat in many a paling park
And bone saws stammer blue smoke as they bite
Into the height of summer. Fall, begin.

II. THE SECOND EQUINOX

Perambulating his green wards, the tree
Warden sees summer's ashes turn to fall:
The topmost reaches first, then more, then all
The twigs take umbrage, publishing a sea
Of yellow leaflets as they go to ground.
Upon their pyres, the maples set red stars,
The seal of sickness unto death that bars
The door of summer. Bare above its mound

Of leaves, each tree makes a memorial
To its quick season and its sudden dead;

With a whole gale of sighs and heaving head,
Each ash attends to its annual burial.

The warden under a boreal blue sky,
Reminds himself that ashes never die.

III. DECEMBER THIRTY-FIRST

The days drew in this fall with infinite art,
Making minutely earlier the stroke
Of night each evening, muting what awoke
Us later every morning: the red heart

Of sun. December's miniature day
Is borne out on its stretcher to be hung,
Dim, minor, derivative, among
Great august canvases now locked away.

Opposed to dated day, the modern moon
Comes up to demonstrate its graphic skill:
Laying its white-on-white on with a will,
Its backward prism makes a monotone.

In the New Year, night after night will wane;
Color will conquer; art will be long again.

IV. MAY DAY

Help me. I cannot apprehend the green
Haze that lights really upon the young
Aspens in our small swamp, but not for long.
Soon round leaves, as a matter of routine,
Will make their spheric music; and too soon
The stunning green will be a common place.
Sensational today runs in our race
To flee the might of May for willing June.

To reach a bunch of rusty maple keys,
Undoing a world of constants, more or less,
I tread on innocence. The warden sees
In May Day the historical success
Of labor; a safe day for planting trees;
A universal signal of distress.

This gorgeous longer poem, written by L. E. Sissman, was
published in his first book, *Dying: An Introduction*, in 1968, just
three years after his diagnosis of Hodgkin's disease, which would
eventually claim his life in 1976 at the age of forty-eight. He
wrote two other collections before his death, and his *Hello
Darkness: Collected Poems* won the National Book Critics Circle
Award in poetry. Though the specific date of the poem's com-
position is not known and it is impossible to ascertain exactly
when the poem was conceived, it is no great stretch to imagine

that it was written before he learned of his diagnosis; it appears in the first section of the book, well before other poems that more explicitly address his illness.

A close reading of the poem illustrates many of the principles by which the structured language of poetry engenders knowing about illness, of divining its presence from the clues discernible in a sentient relationship to the world around us. Read aloud, it is also a fine example of how poetry quite simply gives sound to sense. Though lymphoma is never mentioned, the titles of the poem and of some of its sections announce tropes of disease: "The Tree Warden" evokes a custodial relationship like those on hospital wards, "A Farewell to Elms" is a pun on the title of Hemingway's famed and tragic modern novel, and "May Day" a blatant plea for succor. Of equal predicating importance, Sissman chooses variations on the sonnet, the received poetic form familiar to most readers as a traditional love poem, as the vehicle for his awakening to the possibility of mortal illness—as if to remind us of the fundamental human truth that in love we also confront its antipode, death. Whether he also means to link his nascent illness to a corruption of the natural world is less clear, though the disordered seasons (ash leaves falling in July, "rusty" maples in May) through which the sections of the poem lead us might suggest so; in this context, the concise references to historical moments of upheaval spanning from the Reformation in the poem's first section ("Now a tree man/Tacks quarantine upon its trunk") to the labor movement in the last ("the historical success/Of labor") might also signify that he perceives himself to be on the threshold of a life-shattering trauma, yet one that humane, visionary intervention could help him to transcend.

If these larger elements of the poem are in these ways alive to the possibilities of illness, then a consideration of its constituent language seems all the more persuasive. The imagery is steeped in medical and even funereal qualities: the premature loss of the elm's leaves, making winter of summer; the trees becoming pyres, alight in their own dying leaves, and their self-made burial mounds; "perambulating" trees (for just a moment, in a brilliantly enjambed line) that seem like dazed patients in the hospital; "the red heart" of the rising sun. The poet's ink, from the very beginning of the poem, changes to the flushed color of fever and blood as "ball-/Point pens all suddenly write red"; color also suggests the poet's emotional temperature later in the poem, with the pun on umber in "The twigs take umbrage," expressing an otherwise unarticulated anger that does not cause illness, but rather arises instinctually in response to its earliest stirrings. Even a December day suggests infirmity to the poet; wan and pale, it is embodied and "borne out on a stretcher."

Despite the poem's acute awareness of looming disease, it does not court death. On the contrary, much in the poem resists the negative connotations we might be tempted to bring into the poem as we digest its images and metaphors. "Ashes never die," muses the tree warden, the pun permitting a kind of playfulness with mortality. Similarly, the long nights of winter do wane, giving way to the heartening lines that read: "Color will conquer; art will be long again." This conclusion is all the more poignant as it emerges from the "modern," "monotone" landscape projected by the moon; Sissman's dream of a healthier postmodern world, vibrant and sumptuous, presciently proposed here, has yet to be fully realized. Here is a cancer patient, before he even truly knows it, who is unashamed of the cry for help, and indeed almost revels in it; though at the end of his song it is finally spring, time for renewal, he refuses the carefree celebration of the maypole and instead insists that we hear "the universal signal of distress" of his May Day. Thus the poem ends not thuddingly and despairingly with death, as we might expect, but rather in a complicated, altered newness, a spring that remains hopeful ("a safe day for planting trees") but in which disease is not invisible or denied—one, perhaps, in which resurrection is possible. The poem's vision of disease coexisting with health resists the postmodern impulse to partition the experience of illness into discrete pieces; it integrates disparate realities in a more complex and thus accurate representation of truth.

Another kind of awareness of impending illness occurs in the following poem by the celebrated poet Marilyn Hacker. Born in 1942, Hacker is the author of nine collections of poetry, most recently *Desesperanto*, published in 2003; she has received numerous awards for her poetry, including the National Book Award and the Lenore Marshall Prize from the Academy of American Poets. In 1993 she was diagnosed with breast cancer, and soon thereafter her collection *Winter Numbers* appeared, which contains the following premonitory poem:

Elysian Fields

"Champs-Elysées of Broadway" says the awning
of the café where, every Sunday morning,
young lawyers in old jeans ripped at the knees
do crosswords. Polyglot Lebanese
own it: they've taken on two more shopfronts
and run their banner down all three at once.
Four years ago, their sign, "Au Petit Beurre,"
was so discreet that, meeting someone there,
I'd tell her the street corner, not the name.
They were in the right place at the right time.
Meanwhile, the poor are trying hard enough.
Outside, on Broadway, people sell their stuff
laid out on blankets, cardboard cartons, towels.
A stout matron with lacquered auburn curls
circles the viridian throw rug
and painted plaster San Martín to hug
a thinner, darker woman, who hugs her
back volubly in Spanish—a neighbor,
I guess, and guess they still have houses.
The man with uncut browned French paperbacks,
the man with two embroidered gypsy blouses
and three pilled pitiful pairs of plaid slacks
folded beside him on the pavement where
there was a Puerto Rican hardware store
that's been a vacant shopfront for two years

may not. There's a young couple down the block
from our corner: she's tall, gaunt, gangly, Black;
he's short, quick, volatile, unshaven, white.
They set up shop dry mornings around eight.
I've seen him slap her face, jerking her thin
arm like a rag doll's—a dollar kept from him,
she moves too slow, whore, stupid bitch . . . "She's
my wife," he tells a passing man who stops
and watches. If anyone did call the cops
it would be to prevent them and their stacks
of old *Vogue*s and outdated science texts
from blocking access to the "upscale bar"
where college boys get bellicose on beer.
"Leave him," would I say? Does she have keys
to an apartment, to a room, a door
to close behind her? What we meant by "poor"
when I was twenty was a tenement
with clanking pipes and roaches; what we meant
was up six flights of grimed, piss-pungent stairs,
four babies and a baby-faced welfare
worker forbidden to say "birth control."
I was almost her, on the payroll
of New York State Employment Services
—the East 14th Street branch, whose task it was
to send day workers, mostly Black, to clean
other people's houses. Five-fifteen
and I walked east, walked south, walked up my four
flights. Poor was a neighbor, was next door,

is still a door away. The door is mine.
Outside, the poor work Broadway in the rain.
The cappuccino drinkers watch them pass
under the awning from behind the glass.

In Hacker's precancer vision of the world, the perfection and
bliss of Elysian fields (the pastoral "heaven" of the ancient
Greeks) are ironically full of a blight she cannot help but witness
all around her; by invoking an idealized version of the afterlife
at its namesake corner of Broadway, she precociously locates
herself among the living dead. Amidst all the scourges of our
moment she catalogues, from violence to drug use to homeless-
ness to poverty, it would seem utterly impossible to avert illness.
Even the very streets are dying, as is starkly evident in dead-on
observations such as "the pavement where/there was a Puerto
Rican hardware store/that's been a vacant shopfront for two
years." Heightening the heartbreaking irony is that the poet's
intense engagement with the afflicted around her is what makes
her susceptible; it is those who deny what they see who seem to
remain protected, immune, as at the end of the poem "the cap-
puccino drinkers watch them pass/under the awning and
behind the glass." These unfeeling, distant observers seem safe
and hermetically sealed off in another world, while the speaker,
in identifying with the poor, and owning her feelings about
them, is brought only into a closer proximity to, and thus a
nascent awareness of, cancer. The poem's moving couplets also
evoke this willingness to become corrupted, to be yoked with
the afflicted, a courageous impulse quite contrary to the repres-

sion and disconnection that our popular myths and metaphors typically tell us cause cancer.

For Hacker, our entire culture's not only tolerating but perpetrating the oppression of minorities and women is potentially carcinogenic. In some sense, the poem proposes that she and all of us may have already lost our souls, even if we are not yet deceased; the diagnosis of depression or cancer or AIDS is just a matter of time, best dispensed with sooner rather than later by embracing the most visibly damaged. Yet it is not so straightforward as that. "'Leave him,' would I say?" Her imagined, self-questioning response to the violence (violence that has no home but a city street to make it more impersonally and conveniently "domestic") epitomizes both her empathic impulse to reach out and her unwilling complicity in the first place. There is a reason that this street corner is so hard to locate, an offhand detail provided at the poem's beginning that assumes greater significance as Hacker confronts us with the difficulty of acknowledging our own latent racism: we do not want to visit this place in ourselves, nor to mingle with this poem's untidy characters. The assailant, after all, is a white man, and his victim, his black wife; their publicly troubled marriage becomes symbolic of America's shameful history of race relations. Yet Hacker, ever attentive to the discomposed body, reflects this painful history back to us with an insightful irony: inverting common, bigoted disease myths that would link contagion of whites to miscegenation, she gives us instead the reality of the wife who is ostensibly ill, agonizing in the grip of white sexual exploitation. Thus she recapitulates her view that tyranny is more truly a source of sickness than is any of our most irrational anxieties. At the same time, Hacker effectively reclaims metaphor as an invaluable tool for investigation into what some might consider epidemiology's exclusive domain.

Despite its sobering depiction of a broken postmodern society, like Sissman's, Hacker's poem also preserves some hope for healing, however slim. She does not surrender entirely to the biostatisticians' predictions about what will happen to us, though she knows the disproportionate burden of disease that falls upon the poor and marginalized. The ringing iambic structure of the poem seems an insistent claim on life; our own heartbeats pound as sonic beauty mingles with horrible abjection. The flowing integrity of her lines accommodates and juxtaposes such diverse characters as "polyglot Lebanese" and "college boys" (with no need at all, in the admirable effort to portray the kaleidoscopic nature of our society, to resort to the pretentiously atomized code-language of so much postmodernist language poetry), suggesting that perhaps we can find some way to live more harmoniously together.

We again glimpse this hopeful refusal of insularity in the "stout matron with lacquered auburn curls/[who] circles the viridian throw rug/and painted plaster San Martín to hug/a thinner, darker woman, who hugs her/back volubly in Spanish—a neighbor." The gesture Hacker depicts is itself comforting, presided over by the silent saint (who is remembered for his kindness to the poor, and whose cloak, torn in half and shared with a beggar, is recalled in the tawdry wares of Broadway's street vendors) as if to receive his blessing, beside a patch of brilliant green that seems to denote *life*. The women, she supposes, are neighbors, and share besides their gender a common language (one which, even if not literally understood by the poet, is comprehended metaphorically in its representation in her poem). The implication, here and echoed in the poem's conclusion (with the poet residing next door to poverty personified), is that neighborliness and community—the very crucible of language and poetry—might at least ameliorate our collective pain.

V

Symptoms

Amore obvious entrée to the disease state would be the onset of symptoms. The rock–hard lump discovered in the breast, the searing pain that shoots from the lower back down the leg, the sudden facial paralysis accompanied by slurring of speech: none of these requires a doctor or an X ray to be understood as malady, even though the specific name of the condition may not as yet be articulated. Yet even the most unpleasant symptoms may prove falsely alarming, or are often not specific enough to declare an illness. Some symptoms may themselves be better understood as illness, such as myofascial pain or chronic fatigue, which may defy medicine's most sophisticated attempts to pinpoint their origins. Still others, which may persist indefinitely such as blindness and deafness and immobility, connote whole cultural identities that transcend the lesser category of illness. Even if symptoms do not provide the kind of clear threshold that seems to be physically crossed in (as is commonly said) "falling" ill, nonetheless they are the next major crossroads in most journeys of illness.

The poems in Lucia Perillo's second volume, *The Body Mutinies*, address with remarkable physicality the body's betrayals (as her title suggests) and were written soon after her diagnosis with multiple sclerosis. Born in 1958, Perillo is the author of two other collections of poetry, and is a recipient of a MacArthur Foundation "genius" grant. In the next poem, symptoms of her illness fuse with ideas about the body's representation in art—and humor, as well as religion, become equally valuable modalities for imagining what is happening to her:

Retablo with Multiple Sclerosis and Saints

Saint Joseph for the good death,
Camillus for protection against sickness of the feet.
And Saint Liberata, whose miraculous beard
sprouted to save her from being married to a king—
for when marriage delivers the wrong god in its machine,

however splendid he appears. Then soon your husband
stops taking his meds, and then he's coming down
with visions; your pores smoking like a fleet
of ancient Cadillacs. Late nights find him studying you
—wrench in his one hand and knife in the other—

torn between demolition and repair. Saint Veronica,
patron of hemorrhage, Raphael the Archangel of escape . . .
I'm guessing now about by what miracle's grace

you flew from that coop to this coop of a room
where I'm watching your brush work the latest version

of your face: this one jowled like a yam and floating
where a black cloud threatens to digest your legs.
And it's making me shaky, as if we've boarded a train
whose engineer passed caution three fingers of whiskey ago.
From here, we're riding the caboose full of stumblers.

Each night I try to memorize the fit of my own legs
in case my waking finds them shadowy and numb;
I don't want any limb to think I am ungrateful
for swimming lengths of the ice blue pool.
Or for the soup spoon's lifting, or for the swallowing . . .

I remember the Strait of Juan de Fuca's thundering
(San Juan, patron of baptism, patron of water)
when my bladder opened like a floodgate.
No one was there to watch me rinse in the sea, but still
that moment glimmered with how wildly someday we might float:

jellyfish, medusas, for whom the lighthouse
is just a shadow darkening the voyage on bright days.
But the clouds were flat and blatant—
like clouds in religious iconography, pedestals
for the retablo's apparition swooping down

to save us. And with a wet hem slapping at

my knees, I thought of Frida Kahlo, whose long skirt
hid a withered leg and one foot crushed
when the bus she was riding got hit by a train
and a piece of it came out, good christ, between her legs.

In her self-portraits, I always see
the mirror turned back on this event: Frida shedding tears
or bandaged, Frida bartering her form's grotesqueries,
Frida never letting the body's trauma match
the dispassion worn so stiffly on her face—like a dog

wearing one of those broad, clownlike ruffs
so it can't gnaw or even see what's going on below.
Like the game she loved: Cadavre Exquis.
On folded paper, each player sketches one part
of a figure, so when the whole is finally displayed

the joke lies in discovering the body's sum.
Kahlo always drew genitals—big and pronged
and dripping cum or loopy; she knew
we're always being sucked into that center
around which all this other business spins—

Painting, Poetry, Marx, God.
The unfolded life is uglier than we planned
but the genitals are *exquisite*, they are such
strange flowers, carnivorous & tropical.
And they will die if they can't eat.

Symptoms

Today I read that Kahlo's art has become
the rage, inflated, one of her self-portraits auctioned off
for more than a million bucks. The critic
called those two hundred replications of her face
a self-indulgence—doesn't everybody live with some degree

of pain? *Well, true enough*, I'm thinking as I watch
your brush steer your own flying head through space,
but christ, Viv: by the end she only had one fucking leg!—
How was she supposed to paint the world if she couldn't
even stagger round the block? And I am sick

of the way the miracles have all been relegated
to those TV shows that come on after ten o'clock at night,
when the soul ascends into its reenacted crib of light
above the operating table, while the camera jiggles
until far-flung America comes dialing in. How cute the angels

have become out there, how quaint the Virgin's intercession.
Meanwhile the saints stand nicknamed in the halls
of hospitals where the doctors are such screw-ups
even death gets botched. But here in your workroom
let's throw in Saint Rita: our lady of the last ditch,

impossibility's patron. Whose name can't help
conjuring a waitress in the only diner left in town
and the waterfalling of a bellied pot, the coffee
caught forever in one-half a perfect lancet arch

in our sloppy and hungover visions of being saved.

What we need, my friend,
is that Rita kind of salvation, a miracle
trapped in the crudest grace.
No need for shapeliness or color.
No need for lines converging at a point in space—

just the saint
and the body
and the story that ends with the body raised.
And a few words to tell the story of the story
scrawled at the bottom of this (albeit crude) tin plate.

Reading this stupendous poem is akin to interpreting a great painter's masterpiece, so full of rich imagery and symbolism that we could stare at it for hours—and it is all the more remarkable in its visual sumptuousness when we remember that the poet's illness, multiple sclerosis, often blurs vision and distorts the perception of color in those whom it afflicts. The poet begins by brilliantly situating herself outside of the act of creating art, sidelined by her symptoms as she watches her interlocutor paint—and yet, at the same time, coming away with her own transcendent art in the words of the poem. Her identity soon merges with that of the renowned painter Frida Kahlo, linked as they are by both ethnicity (Perillo is of Mexican extraction) and disability, first sensed at the moment of a bout of incontinence ("And with a wet hem slapping at/my knees, I thought of Frida

Kahlo, whose long skirt/hid a withered leg and one foot crushed"), and even more acutely developed later in the poem ("by the end she only had one fucking leg!—/how was she supposed to paint the world if she couldn't/even stagger round the block?"), in lines themselves so vertiginously enjambed we actually feel what an unsteady gait must be like; the stanza break between ". . . And I am sick//of the way miracles . . ." only heightens this sense, and feels like tripping and falling over the very word, "sick," that names her physical condition.

Needless to say, the two (Perillo and Kahlo, mirrored by the poet's persona in the poem and her friend) are also joined in their gripping use of art to respond to the disturbed body. Though she is suffering, the poet does not meekly pray to the saints to be made well. Rather—with the at once terrifying and funny phrase "torn between demolition and repair" echoing through her (perhaps an allusion to God's creation of Eden, out of which he decides to cast the sinfully self-aware Adam and Eve), she makes her poem an enactment of the tension between these two poles of artistic exploration. She seems to ask: By making it available to others, does the irresistible impulse to make poetry obliterate the genuine, intensely personal pain of the illness experience, or does it assuage it? Does writing poetry in the first place risk, or even invite, destruction by the crippling disease by supplanting standard religious or biomedical interventions—or does it offer instead the best chance to put oneself back together again?

As though responding herself to Viv's unmedicated, all-too-real husband who drives her to what seems like the safety of painting, Perillo at first turns instead, more practically, to a more earthbound "audience": she looks into *herself*. Melding poetry and prayer, she speaks patiently, almost reverently, to her own limbs, entreating them to continue to function normally, as if trying to reason with an internal madman. When she worries her legs might go numb in the night, bargaining with God in the way any of us might, she thinks, "I don't want any limb to think I am ungrateful/for swimming lengths in the ice blue pool./Or for the soup spoon's lifting, or for the swallowing . . ." She clearly recognizes the consoling beauty of the divine, and expresses her own manner of devotion throughout the poem. Yet just as the retablos of her poem's title are folk art imitations (or revisions) of religious iconography, in the end she audaciously proposes herself as her own higher power. Playing the same game of creating human bodies out of drawings of individual parts that Kahlo so loved, she becomes a benevolent, forgiving, and permissive deity, candidly conceding sexuality's preeminence at the center of human existence. She is not even afraid to use Christ's name in vain as she laments Kahlo's awful, almost rapelike accident. The poem allows her to speak the unspeakable, then to imagine the unimaginable; goddesslike, she is empowered in the realm of the poem to determine fate. The contorted bodies she goes on to describe, incongruous, priapic, and "uglier than we planned," are created in her own decrepit, imperfect image, and yet remain very much worthy of veneration, and even love.

Though for Viv art may seem to serve as a kind of escape, from a marriage made turbulent by mental illness, for Perillo it thus becomes a vehicle for transcending the symptomatic body's limitations. She is anything but the passive, paralyzed "victim" of a disease brought on by wantonness, or excess, or any other of the old metaphors' bugaboos; neither does she propose herself as a "poster child" for the MS community. Rather, in the medium of the poem, biology and culture are complexly interwoven; her weak, disabling muscles become beautiful, gliding jellyfish; the shame of urinary incontinence, a kind of blessed self-baptism. Art is indeed miraculous, the depictions of the saints she catalogues in their retablos themselves evidence of its transforming power—both literally, as religious painting intends, but also metaphorically, as expressed by this gifted poet, who coaxes an unexpected and liberating humor from their dour presences, as well as tremendous beauty.

Like Kahlo, Perillo is an artist of the highest order: she offers herself as a conduit between what we know from experience and what we imagine—through faith and magic, dreams and desire—can alter it. She is both iconoclast and herself imbued with a sacred vision, one in which the body itself is not profane but raised to the level of the most holy. Perillo (and her self-incarnation as art's healing potential) allows for a flawed world in which we are all saints—even the invalid or the freak or the unbeautiful, as reinforced by bearded Saint Liberata's reminder that the mortal yet saintly Kahlo often painted herself with coarse facial hair. This "flawed" world is a more inhabitable world in which "perfect" saints and the imperfection of multiple sclerosis share top billing, as in the poem's at once lovely and clumsy title.

Even as she concludes that the true source of salvation is in living human self-expression, more so than in stale dogma, the poet renews the deep connection between poetic utterance and prayer. The beatific saints she lists at the poem's outset fail to protect her, yet the ungainly poem itself seems to restore. It is as though Perillo intends that those who read this poem, like penitents visiting the shrine of the Virgin of Lourdes or lighting candles to patron saints, be just as miraculously healed. Art is her God; "a few words to tell the story" (a reference to the poetically abbreviated textual narratives that underlie the images of retablos), her salvation. What poetry vanquishes is the falsehood of "disease as castigation"; what it renews is the human spirit.

This possibility of healing despite evident symptoms is also considered from a different vantage point in "The Widow's Lament in Springtime," one of the best-known poems by William Carlos Williams. Williams, who lived from 1883 to 1963, hardly needs any introduction, as he is roundly considered, along with the likes of Emily Dickinson and Walt Whitman, an inventor of American poetry, a physician-poet who in his work straddled the border between modernism and postmodernism. Here in his poem the speaker is an observer of symptoms, himself only indirectly affected:

The Widow's Lament in Springtime

Sorrow is my own yard
where the new grass
flames as it has flamed

often before but not
with the cold fire
that closes round me this year.
Thirtyfive years
I lived with my husband.
The plumtree is white today
with masses of flowers.
Masses of flowers
loaded the cherry branches
and color some bushes
yellow and some red
but the grief in my heart
is stronger than they
for though they were my joy
formerly, today I notice them
and turned away forgetting.
Today my son told me
that in the meadows,
at the edge of the heavy woods
in the distance, he saw
trees of white flowers.
I feel that I would like
to go there
and fall into those flowers
and sink into the marsh near them.

The scientifically analytic power of Williams's mind always
seems to predominate when he writes poems, even those that

address the most formidable of emotions arising in the people who occasionally find their way into his verse. (In photographs of the great poet, one can almost envisage the thought waves emanating from his bald, doctorly pate.) Written in 1921, before the advent of such high-tech wonders as MRI scanning and genetic manipulation, the poem shows us the overpowering cerebral discipline that once was so necessarily embodied in a superior diagnostician. Williams is famous for his exact recording of experience; such impure matters as faith rarely if ever attract his attention. Here, it is the repetition of the phrase "masses of flowers" that so vividly, precisely evokes what the subject of the poem is actually seeing, as if through a camera's lens. What is even more striking about this poem, however, is the manner in which the mind itself is also actively imaged by the poet; the repetition embodies the distraction of the grieving mind, laid bare as just another interesting biological phenomenon as it rerecords each detail in its preoccupation, too sad to reflect upon the funereal quality of the image, perhaps unconsciously protecting itself from any such painful association. The line break "I lived with my husband./The plumtree is white today" is heart-wrenching in its familiarity as we watch the mind deflect itself from some unspoken agony, rendered adroitly in the text via the non sequitur. Yet even as it attempts its empathic gesture, this poetry falls short of provoking our own tears; if we feel anything, it is not so much the heaviness of going on with one's life after loss as admiration for the poet's incisiveness and technique. Isolating the symptom preempts our embrace of its source.

Of course, the overall mood of the poem is depressed as it goes about demonstrating the tedious scanning of a world suddenly devoid of emotional resonance by the aggrieved mind. The poem is not at all *overtly* sad, or in more extreme terms, sentimental, which some critics have argued is its greatest strength. What's more, this poem does not simply evoke the things accessible to it by its senses—it goes a step further in attempting to objectively represent a certain evanescent quality of the perceiving mind, strictly refraining from interpretation or elaboration. It is not art in the sense that Perillo's poem is, delighting in the rich conflict between what is real and what is imaginable, allowing us to be ugly and imprecise—it seems instead to aim for a momentary perfection, to pin down the psychic location of hurt, to certify what is woundedness. Even emotion is presented as just another object or thing one might come across, but in the mental landscape—the parallel of the landscape in the poem and the content of the subject's mind having been introduced with the astounding, world-melding opening line, "Sorrow is my own yard." As in most of his poetry, Williams proves himself adept at showing us the mind caught in the act of perceiving, only this time the "thinking brain" itself is more frankly objectified, capable of giving rise to a corresponding set of untrammeled impressions in the reader's mind.

What remains somewhat problematic here, though, is that the impartial distance of the clinician-observer almost completely usurps the purpose of the poem; the same quality that makes the writing stand out proves ultimately to be the final product's greatest difficulty. The heart's song is all the more conspicuously absent since this poem is, after all, about the death of the poet's father—a matter of fact Williams mentions offhandedly in several sources after it was published. Little comfort is provided to the poet's mother, who is literally given over to her grief as she imagines sinking into the marsh of the poem's conclusion. The affective is almost wholly sublimated in the merely topographical; in his ambitious effort to discern what is essential in the experience of sadness, Williams retools the nascent roentgenographic technology of his time: he achieves at best a crude or incomplete image of us that ultimately does not bear out the promised power of his method. He does not even extend to his mother the sympathy that might be her life-line, so intent is he on documenting accurately her mental perceptions. While to "reach out" in this way might violate the poet's modern, innovative approach of recording only what is fleetingly observed, such inflexible calculation also leaves a significant void. At the very least, this deficiency in Williams's work prompts us to consider again, from a vantage point distinct from those we have encountered in Sissman's, Hacker's, and Perillo's poems, the following question: What modulating part, if any, might the emotional response to the generation of sensory data by the body (that is also the flesh), or scientific data by medicine, play in illness—and in turn, in poetry that engages illness?

Williams does approach the sensual at the end of the poem, almost in spite of himself, as his subject imagines herself to be subsumed in the marsh. Similarly, the flaming grasses provide an echo of spent passion; Williams is so attentive that he even has his subject appear unconsciously to choose descriptive terms that reflect the emotions she presumably finds too painful to recall directly. Yet the veiled suicidal gesture also occurring here is not urgently eloquent enough to move this poet to embrace the utter humanness of our mortality—the murky marsh of the soul's perdition, for a moment indulgent of old-style negative metaphoric thinking, seems too dark to penetrate, even for the well-honed instrument of his perspicacity. This "flat-footedness"—by a stretch, analogous to Williams's quasi-scientific metrical innovation, his so-called variable foot, which allowed him to validate his unconventional, arrhythmic line structure— in the end does disproportionate justice to the intellectual component of experience, leaving the reader physically and emotionally unsatisfied. The reader never hears the subject's cadenced sobbing; if he feels his own heart bursting, it is in the vacuum of Williams's steadfast objectivity. Williams remains consummately removed to the bitter end, even as he stands at the yawning edge of his father's grave. Nary a wheelbarrowful of emotion is carried to the poem's abrupt conclusion; the empathetic gesture, though graphed, is never fulfilled. Rather, upon each rereading the poem becomes more and more like a dispassionate case description of depression lifted from a psychiatry textbook—or like the black-and-white slide projected during an endocrinology lecture of a naked subject with a stark black bar across the eyes, meant only to elucidate a specific disease entity, not a human being.

This studied avoidance of what might tritely be referred to as "feelings" as they pour forth from the physical body may indeed have derived in part from Williams's medical training. Even now my profession remains all too hostile to the recognition, or worse yet, the expression of, "feelings" of any sort. The language of poetry has little currency in our great teaching hospitals; it is too often relegated to the support groups of cancer patients, who are too often only made more ill by the experimental drug protocols in which we enroll them (and which may advance research careers more than they do any new cancer treatments). To master the eighteen disease entities in the differential diagnosis of a patient's constellation of symptoms—even if such knowledge offers no possibility of relief or cure—is considered far more valuable than to be able to sit with that patient and to look quietly at the stars with him through his hospital window; to observe and to describe precisely the rash on another's palms is so interesting and important there is no space or time simply to hold the patient's hand.

So perhaps it is somewhat ironic that Williams is so often invoked as an example of humane medical practice. Is it enough to prompt our admiration that he was able to see how narratives of human suffering could be the basis of an imaginative project even when his creativity seems so hermetically sealed against contaminating human subjectivity? In the warm light of healing poetry, in the end his would seem among the most affectively inaccessible (however trailblazing it may seem in its modernity, however commendable that it came from a doctor) of the foremost American practitioners of the craft.

V I

Diagnosis

At the moment of diagnosis, the whole world stops. With the label the doctor places on the symptoms, pronounced matter-of-factly, it is the most crucial juncture in the story of an illness—when the now-"patient" most risks losing control of his or her narrative. (Indeed, the word "patient" shares its Latin root with "passive.") A medicalized language begins to describe our universal premonitions of death, which are suddenly reinterpreted as "symptoms" suppressed or ignored out of fear or shame. Symptoms themselves are translated into hastily sketched diagrams over the physician's desk, involving details of anatomy and physiology; we are depicted as generic containers, the body's innards an embarrassing, knotty mess, its functions already gone terribly awry. The individual experience is summarily voided, supplanted by a jargony vocabulary that is as unfamiliar and incomprehensible as it is irresistible, one that rings with the confidence of so much scientific data and research, one that claims all the answers before all the relevant questions can even be asked. A double transmogrification occurs: the ailing person becomes a patient, who in turn is yoked helplessly to his or her disease, ready to be fed into the health care assembly line.

It is into this shifting, charged borderland that Tory Dent plunges with fierce intelligence ablaze in the following poem, "Apology to the Doctor." Dent, born in 1958 and living with AIDS since 1990, has published two books of poetry. This poem is from her first collection, *What Silence Equals*, published in 1993; her second book, *HIV, Mon Amour*, was a finalist for the National Book Critics Circle Award.

Apology to the Doctor

The consultation room blurs around us as for a noyade does
    the ocean.
The plate glass window convexes beyond its means
in a last ditch attempt to reach the world,
and the world, empathetically, concaves as a sail pivoted leeward
by our conversation, our ballooned cheeks puffing madly to
    save us.
Lifted like a ghost ship, a slaughtered rabbit, a tray of personal
    effects,
in suspended animation afore such inexplicable refusal the sky-
    cult shows us,
aft the earth which has become a roof, ubiquitous and shoddy,
sheltering a tenement of graves, slaves in a galley.
We navigate by default, for there is no right decision.

Diagnosis

Spotlit by our situation we extemporize some outdated existential
  play,
divulge the way strangers passing en route might,
when sharing the same compartment or guilty Catholic albeit
  at heart
atheist who seeks confession as the most efficient method of
  unburdening.
The souls lean closer, avert their heads to the better ear;
we sense the pressure as if their breathing could be heard.
"I've lost so many patients over the past eleven years." I imagine
their bodies felled with expedience into a pit just beneath us.
When I mention my dead friends I envision a bed of red tulips,
then the nothingness of the pavement, then nothing at all.
We stare into our separate abysses for a moment almost like
  prayer,
but I wonder if either of us prays anymore.
Your office posits itself like a Buddhist shrine,
haunted, thus protected, and stripped of religious innuendo.
The single desk survives on its own, statuary and symbolic:
the desire to heal—a sheet of water eternally poured on the
  octagonal rock.
The two leather chairs of community and isolation:
the desire to heal—a drilling for water; a searching for the doctor.
The body a given, a gift, a limitation, also a mystery
of which there be no end to the cruel suspensions of its mystery.
Over my interiority as if, paradoxically, outside myself
how powerful am I, Doctor? You who know and do not know
  the body,

how powerful are we? Our differences as doctor and patient
fall away like personas instantly absorbed by the industrial carpet.
The mass grave gives a rumble, a volcano threatening activity.
Our ineptitudes, perceived through a stauroscope, form in a
    myriad that crowds us;
The deaths so recent, their faces still excruciatingly fresh in the
    morning,
the throng of their voices pitched at an acoustical intensity
we can no longer hear ourselves think in the locked auditoriums
    of our minds.
We stare instead, thirsty and bewildered, at our stupidity
as if it were a talisman, mesmerized by its depth and black comedy,
of its proportion, gargantuan in authority over our plebeian
    knowledge.
We stare as if our ignorance, like knowledge, were something
    to be applied,
that taken far enough might turn, inadvertently, on a dime into
    luck.

In this verbal tour de force, the poet manages to rewrite the
script of receiving the terminal diagnosis. She recounts the
experience using her own impressive vocabulary, replete with
such daunting words as "noyade," "interiority," and "stauro-
scope." By forcing us to go to the dictionary for help, not only
does she assert her own authority (quite literally), but at the
same time she allows us to taste a bit of the patient's terror of
not knowing what all the words mean. Her capacious lines, as
all-encompassing as Walt Whitman's, make room for everything

that needs to be said, further resisting the clipped monologue of the "I've got bad news for you" medical encounter. Their rippling muscularity makes quick work of the doctor's "power" as she bellows, "You who do and do not know the body." Yet even as she thus maintains her bodily integrity, Dent preserves the eerie science-fiction out-of-body flavor of hearing bad news: by peppering the poem with details imbued with scientific qualities—voices are pitched at an "acoustical intensity," the carpet is sterilely "industrial," adjectives like "convex" become weird fun-house-mirror verbs—she transports us into the heart of a nightmare, all the more frightening because it is so uncannily real.

Ingeniously, she captures numerous other facets of this heart-stopping interaction. The symbolism one sees in everything at the moment of diagnosis is all the more poignantly brought to life as the afflicted poet recognizes not so much inevitable death as the complicated possibility of healing. After bearing such discomfiting associations as the "slaughtered rabbit," with its slyly disapproving reference to vivisection (the life-taking means by which science has achieved some of its therapeutic power), and the sinking ship (all the blowing into its sails proves unable to save it), the doctor's office finally becomes a contemplative Buddhist shrine, a place for worship and poetry. Its desk "survives on its own/statuary and symbolic:/the desire to heal—a sheet of water eternally poured on the octagonal rock," the "chairs of community and isolation:/the desire to heal—a drilling for water, a searching for the doctor," plain objects hopefully animated, are enlisted in her protection, in a kind of more humane inversion of Williams's objectifying impulse.

Thus Dent immediately sees past society's injurious assumptions of AIDS = death. She receives her diagnosis as a gift, as an opportunity for knowing, an occasion for imagining healing. In the poem's ethereal space, she is freed from the constraints of how one is supposed to respond to a mortal threat. She is already thinking toward how her changed health status connects her to a living community, envisioning the meaning of her new self, and the possibilities for wellness contained therein, as well as the isolation that awaits her, as this new community is undeniably a stigmatized one. Her equanimity—she is never resigned, nor broken down—as expressed in beautiful, brainy, complex metaphors, is both astonishing and moving.

Perhaps even more compelling here is the poet's exploration of the elusive meaning of empathy. According to her title, the poem is an apology, as though it were necessary to defend or to excuse feeling what the doctor does not. Ironically, she empathizes with *him*, understanding why he cannot save her and even consoling him on the loss of his patients in the face of her own diagnosis. Eventually, their doctor and patient personas are shed, to dissolve into the consultation room's gray carpeting. The intimacy of these two human beings, even across all the cacophonous interference of the postmodern world of HIV test results and "personal effects" and "outdated existential plays" (a deliberate dark joke, as in existentialism nothing can become truly obsolete), is generously proposed in "The souls lean closer, avert their heads to the better ear;/we sense the pressure as if their breathing could be heard"—perhaps the quietest moment in the poem. "We stare into our separate abysses," she adds later, knowing that each one's experience of loss is at once utterly the same and entirely unique. She places herself and her doctor, and so all of us, soundly upon the common ground of poetry—more noble than pity, what she asks of us instead is simply our mindful presence, joining with her in the act of thinking and feeling, of struggling to be, unencumbered by clichés and pretexts and qualms. I know of no better definition of empathy.

The poet Alicia Suskin Ostriker, in a sequence of poems she bluntly titles "The Mastectomy Poems," also considers the impact of learning her own diagnosis, that of breast cancer. Born in 1937, she is the author of nine volumes of poetry, including *The Little Space*, which was a finalist for the Academy of American Poets Lenore Marshall Prize, and *The Crack in Everything*, which was a finalist for the National Book Award and in which this sequence (from which the poem below is excerpted) appears.

Riddle: Post Op

A-tisket, a-tasket
I'm out of my casket
Into my hospital room
With a view of Riverside Drive
Where the snow is a feathery shawl
My children plump as chestnuts by the fire
My son-in-law so humorous and tall
My mate grandly solicitous, a broker

With a millionaire's account.
My friends bob in
And out like apples
Crying and crying *You look wonderful*
While underneath this posh new paisley
Bathrobe that laps me in luxury
Underneath my squares of gauze
I've a secret, I've a riddle
That's not a chestful of medals
Or a jeweled lapel pin
And not the trimly sewn
Breast pocket of a tailored business suit
It doesn't need a hanky
It's not the friendly slit of a zipper
Or a dolphin grin
Or a kind word from the heart
Not a twig from a dogwood tree
Not really a worm
Though you could have fooled me
It was not drawn with a crayon
Brushed on with watercolor
Or red ink,
It makes a skinny stripe
That won't come off with soap
A scarlet letter lacking a meaning
Guess what it is
It's nothing

In Ostriker's poem, deceptively simple language, reminiscent of a child's nursery rhyme, deliberately re-creates the infantilization of the patient in the face of a crushing diagnosis. It almost seems to become a plea for a kind of primal language, one's very first learned words, which came before the corrupting influence of coercive, programmatic narratives about death and disease acquired later in life. The poem shines with bold, unadorned imagery; bared almost entirely even of the trappings of punctuation, it becomes a kind of picture book of the process of finding out what her body contains, as if after her mastectomy she were so totally diminished—returned to the physically helpless and presexual state of childhood—that she *must* learn to read all over again, to reassert adult mastery over both body and word. She descends through layer after layer of protective and obfuscating metaphor and imagery, until she reaches beneath her robe and under her gauze bandages, finally staring at the wound that has been so carefully obscured from her view. Her willingness to be playful (and also, by implication, vulnerable) stands in sharp contrast to the actual solution to the poem's ostensible riddle: it rhymes with "answer," she might have said, and yet it—cancer—remains unspoken. Almost mischievously, she refuses to say the word—or *their* word, the word which is not merely a word but a diagnosis, with all its enforced meanings. Where Dent demands explanation and empathy, Ostriker seems actually to prefer silence.

This silence, however, is decidedly on her own terms. In her cascade of disparate but each equally compelling images—

"That's not a chestful of medals/Or a jeweled lapel pin/And not the trimly sewn/Breast pocket of a tailored business suit"— she makes it perfectly clear that she knows what she has, and that it is just as important, maybe even more so, that she exert control over this information. The next line, "It doesn't need a hanky" tells us very frankly what we can do with any pity we might feel for her. This adamant denial is really about who gets to tell the story of her illness, and when it will be told. If there is something of an honest admission of fear too, or of revulsion (or at least an acknowledgment of the kind of damaging thinking about illness Sontag critiques), it is expressed in the lines "Not really a worm/though you could have fooled me," as if the wholesome apple suggested in the image of her healthy visiting friends were in her own case infested, or in "It makes a skinny stripe/That won't come off with soap," which evokes the pernicious association of illness and uncleanliness. By the end of the poem, her pronouncement that "It's nothing," which at first blush might suggest that she has been completely ravaged by her cancer, eaten away to nothingness, becomes an affirmation of her intent to be healed. Perhaps also it simply expresses rage, pure and unfiltered, that the child-voice she adopts in the poem has license to "get away with."

Ostriker, like Dent, refuses to have her illness narrative told to her. On the contrary, she reverses the expected order of things, taking charge and sitting us right down on her lap as she begins to tell it to us—wittily and allusively, using words withheld as much as those she puts on paper, instead of with steely scientific precision. The metaphors she chooses are truly her own; we might think we know this fairy tale, with its blighted fruit and bittersweet ending, but it is about to be retold. The "scarlet letter" that marks her "has no meaning" in this poem, and thus, in rejecting the moral and religious stigmas associated with Hawthorne's *The Scarlet Letter*, the poet must create a new meaning—a novel metaphor, one that eschews transgression and shame. Her illness, instead of setting her back in an old world of female disempowerment, becomes the locus for a healthier cultural production.

Indeed, the choice of the poem as the medium for the telling, ancient gathering place of voices, first act of community-building, is itself important: she proves to us that language can be reinvented, that through it illness can be reclaimed as not only conscionable but endurable. Like all of these poets, by her use specifically of the language of poetry she is proclaiming that her illness belongs to us all, in our various guises as lovers, witnesses, care providers, and fellow sufferers. She invites us to participate in her infirmity—who among us can expect to escape illness?—and in so doing she is liberated of all the baneful attitudes about disease that modern medicine has done much less to refute. At the same time, she unifies us across the disjointed landscape of our cultural moment. Superstition is dispelled by song, and lack of mutual understanding (in spite of our ever-expanding ways of knowing) is just another reason to carry on, and to write the next poem.

A Theory of Illness
Narrative: "June S."

One of my favorite poems about illness was written by a woman whose full name I do not even know, who I suppose has never published a book or been critically reviewed, identified only by the probable pseudonym of "June S." Clipped neatly from what must have been a small-town newspaper article, it was given to me a few years ago by a medical intern I once supervised, a brilliant young woman who has since gone on to become one of our chief residents, and who plans to go on eventually to a career in oncology, with the almost unheard-of and decidedly *un*sexy sub-subspecialty of palliative care. (I remember fondly our early morning conversations about poems, and other artistic and imaginative responses to illness, from Margaret Edson's long-running play *Wit* to Mitch Albom's best-seller *Tuesdays with Morrie*—warm, delicious consolations over the hospital cafeteria's perennially bad coffee and half-stale donuts.) The poem is tacked to the corkboard above my office desk, and I reread it almost every morning before I start my work with patients. I feel as though the poet is speaking directly to me, that she is telling me something that is invaluably, ineffably true.

It takes me only a few seconds to read it; somehow its author's anonymity deepens its meaning for me, allowing me to imagine what she looks like, to picture whether she is black or Asian or white, how she touches the woman sitting beside her in the cancer survivor group, whether she has for company and solace a husband or children who bring her breakfast in bed, or a wind-combed golden retriever she walks on some misty, rock-strewn beach in Maine, or simply a transistor radio tuned to NPR on the kitchen table in a small apartment, its antennae angled toward an open window as if reaching out for contact with the hopes and dreams of the outside world. The poem itself seems to me like the window onto the limitless narrative possibilities such an engagement with illness makes possible. Yet it is also just a moment in time, a very particular pause in the business of life: Though I've only had it for three or four years, the paper on which June's poem is printed has already turned a disconcerting orangy yellow.

The poem's abbreviated, almost hurried quality—the lines themselves are very short, and it is only about a dozen lines long—always makes me wonder too whether the poet has undergone a mastectomy, and whether she means to echo the curt, to-the-point dialogue of the surgeons who may have buzzed over her bed, intent on their own narrative of her cancer. I imagine these doctors trying to discharge her from the hospital as soon as possible, struggling to balance some vestigial concern for her well-being against the pressures of attending to countless other patients, wanting to be back in the OR to learn how to improve their surgical techniques, and worrying about the hospital's huge budget deficits (and maybe their own employment) in the face of declining reimbursements. Maybe the poet means to reinterpret even the surgery itself, its neat row of stitches, its efficient and parsimonious commerce with her body, her poem like the scalpel, unerring, precise, and searingly direct. More ominously, I wonder if its brevity is somehow symbolic of her prognosis, a "six months to live" pronouncement from an imperious oncologist sometime down the road that relegated her to the support group she describes. Of course, all of these possibilities could merely be accidental, or the products of an overzealous imagination—and yet every day I reread her poem and can't help believing, in the end, that she is still alive.

Just like some of the poems by the widely published and critically acclaimed "professional" poets I have presented thus far in this book, June's work offers clues just as crucial to the larger understanding of illness, of its meaning in human terms. Just like the poems tacked to the makeshift memorials to the victims of the September 11 tragedy, this small fragment of language imagines persistence and renewal in spite of destruction. Like David standing down Goliath, June's diminutive poem has the power to fell the entire gigantically distorted monstrosity of what health care in twenty-first-century America is becoming. The poem is itself a metaphor, which can in turn stimulate more "out of the box" thinking so urgently needed in medicine.

Perhaps at this pivotal point suggested by June's poem, poised between a defining, irrevocable confrontation with disease and its eventual denouement, we might begin to consider an empiric theory of illness narrative, one that has already started to take shape as we ponder what we have learned from the poems discussed thus far. "We stare as if our ignorance, like knowledge, were something to be applied,/that taken far enough might turn, inadvertently, on a dime into luck," says Tory Dent, in her hypercritical yet cautionary way, and she is quite correct to question the substantive reaches of empathy. Might the wish to be more empathetic weaken our faculties of critical thinking and self-determination? She seems to be arguing that empathy is an inexact tool, which in spite of its imperfect nature can still redirect us toward the right path, as if to some extent by chance. Surely she remains even more wary of the usual ways of comprehending illness, which motivate her own work and the search for the larger, more humane alternative she herself finally proposes.

From my own idiosyncratic vantage point as both a physician and a poet, and from my ongoing close reading of poetry that arises from the experience of illness—not to mention years of defending myself against some physician colleagues who view poetry with disdain and even suspicion (and even some fellow poets, who reflect this purely modern antipathy between science and art upon me in the other direction)—I have sensed out firsthand the following set of principles by which I believe poetry may indeed exert a powerful therapeutic force for the afflicted, abetting and sustaining an assured and self-actualizing response to suffering. This poetic response is not bound by the

A Theory of Illness Narrative: "June S."

familiar old metaphors which have long poisoned our thinking about illness, even as it draws on the oldest of expressive art forms. Nor are these narratives self-consciously erected as defenses against the postmodern deconstruction of the body and community, even though they go a long way toward repairing these fractures. On the contrary, as we have seen in the preceding poems, poetry is a wellspring for fresh metaphors that reconsider illness in radically new ways, and it deploys itself in relation to disease by joining us viscerally in one body and vocally in one community.

I hasten to add that I have not yet resorted to writing poems on my patients' prescriptions instead of the names and doses of antiretrovirals for AIDS patients, say, or pegylated interferon for chronic hepatitis C patients, or any other of a number of other drugs that physicians employ because we hope they might help but that we know have less than completely curative effects. It would be irresponsible to assert that poetry cures diseases—just as it would be irresponsible for me to make that claim for Laetrile or snake oil, or even AZT. Yet as I have shown, I do engage many of my patients in a program of relevant reading that I believe educates and nourishes me as much as it does them. It affords us opportunities to enter a more broadly defined process of healing—to value coping with disabling pain, say, or confronting paralyzing fears of death—as much as it seeks to eradicate tumor cells or shrink arteriosclerotic plaques. (And incidentally, I can always joke, even really bad poetry has none of the toxic side effects so many other treatments do!)

So here is a kind of oversimplified, practical list, with the admission up front that to rigorously test (according to modern statistical methodology such as the randomized controlled trial) any of these proposed mechanisms of action would be difficult indeed. Tests of their emotional soundness, if any could ever be devised, might show them to be antistatistically insignificant. I should note, however, that some of these notions are well accepted in psychiatric and behavioral medicine circles; poetry therapists (and other licensed expressive arts practitioners) routinely employ them, consciously and unconsciously, in their invaluable work with their clients.

Any experienced care provider has observed the therapeutic effect of simply *assigning a name* (and not necessarily a medical diagnosis) to the disquieting symptoms and signs with which a patient presents; imagine amplifying that effect by allowing the patient to discover and to name for himself or herself what the affliction is. Indeed, whether the name is a specific diagnosis is almost irrelevant, as the Ostriker poem demonstrates: rather, it is the process of self-definition that seems to promote healing. Poems most precisely name illness experience, mixing medical and scientific terms with visceral, emotional language. (The act of naming assumes all the more importance in our postmodern moment, when elsewhere clear-cut definitions and meaningful conclusions elude us—recall the slasher-film killer who is resurrected time and time again for unending sequels, or the soap opera star who dies but then again does not to keep a plotline going indefinitely.) Because the poem commands a diverse audience, the naming it achieves implies partnership between reader and poet, doctor and patient, community and individual—it is not imposed like a death sentence, but rather is arrived at as a consensus.

For all the talk about metaphors that infuses analyses of illness, it is important to recall what a metaphor actually is, and not necessarily just in the limited Aristotelian sense. *Creating metaphors* in poetry (or in storytelling more generally) is itself in fact a process similar to the healing process, involving an imaginative translocation from one state or position to another. In the construction of metaphor, emotional intelligence participates most directly in our thinking, pairing unlike objects or ideas— and from the energy of their friction, we are propelled toward an entirely new conclusion. Schmaltzy examples come too easily to hand: the sun can become desire, the mud in the river a sadness, or conversely, the joy in a child's eye pure light, yet even these move us to a small degree. While some illness metaphors are, as in Sontag's analysis, plainly destructive, in much of contemporary poetry written about illness, the opposite is true.

The poem, in its rhythms and rhymes, metaphorically might *restore the sufferer's sense of control* over deranged bodily functions. Recall the pounding iambic heartbeat in Marilyn Hacker's poem, helping to soothe us even while exposing the sordid innards of an unhealthy, oppressive culture; recall the deliciously long-winded lines of Tory Dent's poem, which spool out across the abbreviated, breathtaking moment of her diagnosis, allowing her (and her reader) to swim in the numerous possibilities of her changed self. The poem becomes a kind of stethoscope through which the patient can auscultate and describe the rhythms of her own heart. The poet may re-create the integrated self in the surefooted movement of the writing, or sew back together the fragments of a sense of self torn asunder by exisional biopsy and allograft transplant.

At the same time, poetry places the patient in direct *communication* with others who have suffered with a disease, across centuries and across cultures. This kind of communication has become dear, in the face of science's arrogant efforts to stamp out what it indiscriminately and contemptuously considers "old wives' tales," and amidst present-day culture's stunted and often falsely "democratic" languages of e-mail and sound bite. Through the mysterious séance of the poem, L. E. Sissman can argue with Ernest Hemingway; Perillo conjures Kahlo for one last posthumous game of Exquisite Corpse.

Writing poetry specifically and dramatically *establishes the patient's authority* in the setting of illness, an authority so often wrested from him or her by those of us in the medical establishment. I have often thought of poems as variations on the experts' editorials that appear in prestigious medical journals to comment on new data published relating to one disease or another. No greater expertise can be achieved than that which comes from actually living with an illness; poetry harnesses this wisdom, asserting the authority of the afflicted in the most persuasive and incontrovertible of terms, in an idiom that shares its power instead of wielding it like a weapon. We should have any of these poets give readings of their work at hospitals' Grand Rounds, that venerable forum where physicians learn from leaders in their respective fields of clinical or scientific investigation.

A Theory of Illness Narrative: "June S."

Poetry also *empowers through the construction of transformed identity*, as the patient after naming and then authoring his or her illness finally identifies with the illness. This identification is more than the somewhat consoling realization that one is not alone in having chronic pain, or ALS; it is embracing the altered self, reentering the newly sensitized skin, forgiving, even celebrating, the traitorous body. Williams offers a particularly complex and moving example of this transformation, in which the emotional interpenetrates the physical as his subject literally sinks into the swamp of depression, which simultaneously promises renewal in its riot of springtime blooms. The poem accommodates its contrasting moods in a manner that almost defies analysis, so utterly recognizably human is this conflicted state. This changed identity is ultimately the shared identity of being human, familiarly flawed and nuanced, not a raucous call to disease activism; it empowers not by exoticizing or politicizing but rather through empathy.

Perhaps most important, the poem provides a nonjudgmental space to *explore and accept death* as one possible ending to the patient's life story, an outcome medicine remains notoriously inept at helping patients to grasp. As a further outgrowth of the biological compulsion to fashion narratives that explicate what our senses merely report about our surroundings—especially necessary when our senses seem limited or deficient—poems, prayers, and myths relating to death abound in every culture, and are often all we have as a record of how our long-gone ancestors lived. Each of the poets we have considered thus far in some way or other contends with mortality, no matter at what earlier juncture in the illness experience we encountered them. Death is the greatest human drama of all, and as such requires the most profound attention and understanding we can muster, of the sort possible exclusively through poetry.

Finally, the written legacy of poetry not only *teaches* all those who will encounter it about the illness itself, from a perspective different from that found in textbooks, it also preserves the fragile details of the human experience of sickness against all the well-meaning but callous technologies that tend to obliterate them. Teaching students is like caring for the infirm, and as such is critically dependent on empathy. These poems, when shared on ward rounds with medical students and house officers, give permission to questions rarely asked in hospitals, even at the monthly meetings of the medical ethics committee; when shared in a cancer survivor group, they ignite hope. When shared by doctors with their patients, they inspire a conversation that instructs each of the participants in the timeless art of love.

VIII

Treatment

Inevitably, it seems, after the diagnosis comes the treatment—and since the treatment most patients find in today's hospitals is most definitely not poetry, they are often confronted with a dizzying array of technologies and chemicals that are supposed to restore them to health, if not spiritually, then at least physiologically. Our overriding modern healing impulse is to eradicate the infection, to excise the imperfection, to irradiate the tumor—and to ask questions later, if at all. People with cancer or HIV infection who refuse costly and toxic treatment must have their competency to make such perverse decisions evaluated; meanwhile, certain lower-profile or harder-to-define or differently stigmatized conditions such as depression and chronic pain, for which safer, less expensive, and more effective treatments exist, go woefully undertreated. One imagines a time in the not-so-distant past when the doctor's house call was as much a social occasion as a medical intervention, a chance to swap stories about family or give advice about community projects over a glass of lemonade while the prescriptions were doled out; these days, in contrast, just going to a doctor's office has come to imply seeking the latest treatment, one that has perhaps been advertised on TV. (Such apparently lesser interventions as disease education and preventive health measures are now relegated to nurse practitioners or personal trainers or physician assistants.) When considering treatment options, it is as though a specific pathogen or adversary must be identified as a cause and then targeted for elimination; militaristic metaphors for these treatments, perhaps even more objectionable than those in popular culture Sontag derides, abound.

With this kind of adversarial mentality dominating the medical profession—making it often too easy to confuse the patient with the disease, leading to the frankly deleterious misconception of the patient as the enemy—it is not surprising that "alternative" healing has become increasingly popular with the infirm, even among those who also generally subscribe to the biomedical model. Herbal medicines, acupuncture, massage therapy, meditation and biofeedback, and yes, even poetry therapy, to name just a few, are among the various options patients now elect to treat their illnesses more holistically. While support in the form of scientific data used to judge the efficaciousness of standard therapies is sometimes weak or even lacking for these methods, their growing use suggests benefits that such analyses may not yet have discerned, or are not yet even capable of quantifying.

The next poem well illustrates some of these issues surrounding the current treatment of illness. Maxine Kumin, born in 1925, has published twelve books of poetry. Her work has received the Poets' Prize and the Pulitzer Prize, among many other awards. She has served as consultant in poetry to the Library of Congress and poet laureate of New Hampshire, and is a former chancellor of the Academy of American Poets. She is also the author of a memoir of illness, *Inside the Halo and Beyond: The Anatomy of a Recovery* (W. W. Norton, 2000). Her most recent collection of poems, *The Long Marriage,* was published just a year after surviving the carriage accident that nearly took her life; like her memoir, the poems eloquently detail her struggle with disability and chronic pain.

Grand Canyon

Past the signs that say *Stop! Go Back!*
We are friendly Indians! past the tables
of garnet and red rock, of turquoise and silver,
past horses thin as paper, profiled
against a treeless horizon, I come
to where all roads converge, I stand
at each of a dozen jumping-off places
with my fellow cripples, my fellow Americans,
peering into our national abyss.

Outings for wheelchair postulants
are regular affairs here on the brink
of this improbable upheaved landscape;
the clinic for chronic pain my therapists

back East referred me to is,
by Western measurements, just down the road.
The group is quiet. Wind music lobs
endless songs to would-be suicides
from the river bottom's Loreleis,
a redemptive eight-hour hike below us,
but no one's leapt this week. Some travel
both ways on bony backs of mules,
slaves forever on this torturous trail.

Despite the crowds, despite the kitsch,
this mesa, this elevated plain,
has always been on my life-list.
Life-list, a compound noun in my
directory. The fact is, I'm alive.
The fact is, no conjecture can resolve
why I survived this broken neck
known in the trade as the hangman's fracture,
this punctured lung, eleven broken ribs,
a bruised liver, and more. Enslaved

three months in axial traction, in what they call
a halo, though stooped, I'm up. I'm vertical.
How to define chronic pain?
Maddening, unremitting,
raying out from my spinal cord
like the arms of an octopus, squeezing,

Treatment

insidious as the tropic anaconda . . .
The experts are fond of saying
spinal cord injuries are like
snowflakes; no two are ever the same
but while you're lying on the table, unfrocked
—no one tells you this—the twists and pummels,
the stretches and premises are identical.
One size of therapy fits all.

Who practices for this disaster? Who
anticipates that the prized horse will bolt,
that you will die / should have / didn't?

That a year will pass before
you can walk the line they ask the drunk to
on balance on one foot. Who knew
the dumb left hand could be retrained
to cut meat, brush teeth, and yet the day I signed
my name in loose spaghetti loops beneath
the intended line, I wept. We joked
I'd buy a stamp pad, roll my thumb,
someday receive outrageous sums
from Sotheby's for my auctioned print
brave banter we all but choked
on, better than the cant that says,
be grateful you're alive, thank God.
Implicit in it, *you've had it too good.*

> What would the friendly Indians trade
> to break loose from the white man who
> reduced them to servitude?
> What would the suicidal barter
> for deliverance from
> the Sisyphean boulder
> they daily roll uphill?
> What would I trade to regain
> my life the way it was?
> From pillar to abyss
> the answer echoes still:
> The word is *everything*.

Kumin has chosen an apt setting for her meditation on the difficulties of treatment. Trapped in our insular world of focus groups and office cubicles, we are compelled to travel together with her to a distant, resonant, even mythical place if we are to seek even the possibility of relief. Expecting a shrine of healing, an American wonder, instead she encounters only more of the familiar struggle: in the lines "my fellow cripples, my fellow Americans,/peering into our national abyss," she articulates the despair she feels living in what she instantly paints as a corrupt society, manufacturer of disingenuous leaders like Richard Nixon. The echo sent back by the canyon becomes a device to suggest we are all cripples, psychically at least, in the face of such easily parroted sloganeering and facile patriotism. The Grand Canyon, despite all its contradictory well-hyped yet down-home grandeur, opens up to her like an awful gaping wound, its "dozen jumping-off places" an invitation as much to suicide as to recuperation. It is a wound as old as the injustice done by white settlers to the euphemistically tamed Indians, a deep sore which has never healed. Her own injury becomes enmeshed with this one; she has a "hangman's fracture," caused by a carriage accident, conjuring associations we Americans have with the Wild West. Her chronic pain and its treatment— this "outing" itself seems to be intended as therapeutic—are thus contextualized by a history of unredressed, large-scale trauma.

"Go back," the native people tell her, as if offering to her the power of incantation that was their way of healing, or at least warning her away from the precipice to which modern modalities have driven her. Though medicine is quick to cast the uniqueness of her spinal cord injury as glamorous or sexy, when it comes to something as tedious as a treatment plan, the poet dolefully reports, "One size of therapy fits all." The arduous work of her rehabilitation is symbolized by the image of the ride down into the canyon: "Some travel/both ways on bony backs of mules,/slaves forever on this torturous trail," where the patients themselves become beasts of burden. Yet mules are known especially for their stubbornness, and though the opportunity to jump to one's death is all around, all the more enticing in the face of so much beauty into which one might leave pain behind, Kumin remains resolutely alive. She even owns her brokenness, fracturing her lines where neither phrasing, meter, or syntax allows natural breaks, inscribing her stooped posture upon the text itself by enjambing an early line after "I stand," pointing out how her present location is itself disjointed and forced, a compulsory checkmark on her "*Life-list*, a compound noun in my/directory," the mesas pushed up though the earth like bones in a compound fracture poking through skin.

Kumin, renowned as a virtuoso of received poetic forms, surely intends the irony of the persistent disruption of form in this harrowing poem, which is all the more notable as it goes unrepaired even as she describes her treatment. The lines remain awkward and ungainly, like the drunk whose task of walking a straight line she cannot perform either. For all the failings of conventional treatments, the practitioners of which have banished her to this other place because of her lack of progress, she does hint at the therapeutic value of writing: "Who knew/the dumb left hand could be retrained/to cut meat, brush teeth, and yet the day I signed/my name in loose spaghetti loops beneath/the intended line, I wept." The reader feels here that the act of writing is more than just a routine task, like tooth-brushing, and even more than life-sustaining, like cutting meat. Writing is both an act of self-definition—what she first writes is her own name—and a critical step toward recuperation.

The very title of her book, *The Long Marriage*, similarly implies a relationship to chronic pain and its treatment that is ongoing and intimate; her pain is the dear subject of her imagination, written and perhaps even loved into a negotiated if not entirely peaceful coexistence. Because it is into that gorgeous, wrecked landscape that she whispers her fondest desire—that she would give up everything to be herself again. In creating this poem, she seems to have gotten her wish; perhaps she has not been cured according to the physiotherapist's end points, but surely she has healed on her own terms. "Life the way it was" is what she demands; to write another poem, this grand poem, over pain's pitiless objections, seems to satisfy this desire. That she has the imaginative strength to carve her own narrative into the Grand Canyon, to shoulder the immensity of its symbolism as both wound and wonder, only underscores her body's resilience.

The hegemony of curing is so persuasive in modern medicine that we even promulgate treatments for conditions that are normal human states. Menopause is one such example, for which hormone replacement therapy with animal or synthetic estrogens and sometimes progestins has been prescribed, as a matter of routine, to allay the risks of coronary disease and osteoporosis for postmenopausal women. Now we find that the benefits of such treatment are much smaller than had been postulated, while the risk of breast cancer, blood clots, and other morbidities may be dangerously increased. Aging is another case in point, as zealous patent-seeking geneticists comb our chromosomes for possible "cures" for this natural process. In the next poem, Alice Jones proposes a different approach to menopause and aging that makes surprisingly effective use of nothing more than innocuous, low-tech language. A physician herself, she is the author of *The Knot*, a collection of poetry that won the Beatrice Hawley Award and was published in 1992.

Prayer

Send rain, down to the dry bare bones of me,
    the tarsals planted in sand, no sage
    or mint or parsley will grow here, snails
    are sucked dry, leave frail shells
    in the dug garden's dirt, no flowers, no fronds;

Send rain, down to the deep bowl of my pelvis,
    barren red hollow, the empty sack
    sags now with age, the scarred yellow ovals
    discharge their eggs in irregular cycles,
    no longer linked so well to the moon;

Send rain, down to the restless quartered meat
    that thuds on my ribs, whose valves
    measure thin blood as it seeps through
    the pipes feeding desiccated organs,
    whose mortal work forms sludge;

Send rain, down to the small transparent curve,
    the opaque lens that filters dim light
    to the lustrous surface and on to dense
    convolutions of brain, the task of my sighted
    vitreous globes that turn in their padded cells;

Send rain, down to the knots and whorls,
    where memory continues to pile its thick layers,

sloughs surface, and roots reach into
that grey ground where my neurons grow sparse
and leached soil sprouts nothing new.

Send rain.

Though not specifically addressed to a particular illness, this
poem nonetheless reveals an intimate knowledge of the
anatomy and inner workings of the human body while at the
same time preserving a sense of wonder, and perhaps even slight
disgust, at its occult mysteries. The incantatory diction places it
in unobstructed communication with ancient healers' poetry; its
irresistibly sensuous plea for rain, which the poet imagines may
restore the aging body, recalls the Native American view of the
suffering individual as an integral part of the larger natural
world upon which she depends for wellness. The poet repre-
sents the body as open to and available to the elements, almost
starved for them; here, words become a luxurious rainfall, pour-
ing over us in the long sentence fragments that constitute each
stanza. Such a persuasive reminder of this interdependence
between the human organism and our surroundings is itself a
kind of joyful tonic.

The allusion early on to medicinal herbs clearly allies the
speaker with complementary or alternative approaches to healing.
Rather than a toxic treatment that comes from the exploitation
and manipulation of the natural environment (for an illness that
might also be a consequence of human despoiling of nature), Jones
offers the poet's heartening alternative vision of the disquieted

human body taking sustenance while remaining in harmony with the world around her. Indeed, the "leached soil" of her brain, in which nothing will grow, seems not just blunt testimony to the barrenness of the imagination of our current era but also an oblique reference to our patrimony of Love Canal and Chernobyl and Bhopal, and any of the other environmental disasters that go on killing people long after the contamination has occurred. Poetry remembers even as we age, while society seems willing to forget so long as we continue to get cheap power from nuclear plants or bigger tomatoes from chemical fertilizers and pesticides. Sweetly inspiring, cleansing rain, instead of radioactive fallout or poisonous vapors, is what the anti-technology of poetry produces.

Again, as we have seen in many of the other poems, the creation of new and, in this case, literally radical metaphors—we feel our creatural roots grow into this language as the mind becomes reclaimed earth, the pelvis a vessel in which to hold rainwater, the eye sockets protectively padded cells—propels the reader from one state of being to another, from exhausted observer to rejuvenated celebrant. There is a basic human comfort in these lines, a sound wisdom that dispels the anxiety about aging and stabilizes the moodiness of menopause. Indeed, Jones is boldly engaged here in the very act of reimagining our humanity from the depths of the body outward, as if to suggest that the only treatment for our dehumanized condition is to start all over again by making poems. Here, in the magical, bountiful garden of poetry, in the resonant chamber of the body, the physician-poet seems to demonstrate that pure language is all we ever needed to be cured of what ails us.

IX

Side Effects

edicines, surgery, and radiation are each in a very
real sense a kind of permissible violence wrought
on nonconforming, unhealthy, disordered bodies
and minds. So it is not at all surprising that they often lead to
what we rather benignly term "side effects." The blurred line
between aid and injury was not so unclear before the advent of
ether (the first anesthetic for surgery) and antiemetics (to pre-
vent vomiting induced by ingesting medicinal substances),
which made these interventions more tolerable by obscuring
some of their unintended or undesired consequences. Without
such means to make their services more palatable, the earliest
premodern barber-surgeons and physicians were regarded by
many of their peers with suspicion, if not outright fear and hos-
tility—they were often seen as butchers who corrupted the
sacred wholeness of the body, charlatans who bled and poisoned
those who were already debilitated.

Unfortunately, the dreaded side effects from treatments
doctors prescribe have never been entirely erased, even with

the vast improvement of such soothing techniques—and these may have their own side effects, too. The great modernist poet T. S. Eliot, in the famous line from his poem *The Waste Land*, sums up the seismic cultural shift of his time by casting all of human consciousness as anesthetized—a powerful metaphor for numbed imagination and uncritical thinking that still rings true now. Ironically, he was critiquing what today seems an end result of the same modernism he espoused, as a kind of "side effect" from which we might awaken—it was relentless modernist technological advancement that brought such marvels as anesthesia in the first place, which in turn soon bred the mindless reliance on all manner of "amenities" that Eliot so distrusted (and which now seems to have evolved into our addiction to "the next next thing"). Nevertheless, despite his internal inconsistencies, his words remain a wonderful example of poetry's power to transform scientific hubris into something of far more enduring meaning and human value. They also leave us pondering how and why the best of intentions do so frequently result in unforeseen side effects.

So it is often that we think that treatments are worse than the diseases they are directed at, and for yet other good reasons: many thousands of Americans die each year from therapies they receive for diseases they might have lived with far longer if left alone, while countless more are injured or made to feel sicker by treatments that do not actually kill them. Medical error accounts for a high proportion of these tragically premature "iatrogenic" deaths, yet even with better safeguards many could be avoided if only the ill did not accept treatment. People living with illness thus face a daunting dilemma when considering whether to undergo potentially toxic treatments or to take their chances going without them. Alternative therapies, for the most part poorly studied and unregulated, are not without their own dangers and pitfalls, and pose the additional concerns of quackery and knowing exploitation of the infirm. (Treatments using naturally occurring substances will likely remain underinvestigated since they are more freely available and thus not subject to the lucrative patents sought by the pharmaceutical companies for their synthetic drugs.)

In the next poem, we see dramatized some of these conflicts as the patient's course careens from the hope of treatment into unintended adverse effects—all the more moving because for the poet Toi Derricotte, the treatment was imposed rather than offered, and upon a normal condition that, like aging, is too often biomedically pathologized: childbirth. Derricotte was born in Detroit, Michigan, in 1941. Her books of poetry include *Tender* (1997), *Captivity* (1989), and *The Empress of the Death House* (1978). *The Black Notebooks*, a literary memoir, was published from W. W. Norton in 1997. Her honors include the Folger Shakespeare Library Poetry Book Award, and the Lucille Medwick Memorial Award from the Poetry Society of America. Her collection *Natural Birth*, from which the first section of the poem "delivery" below is taken, was initially published in 1983 and rereleased in 2000.

delivery

i was in the delivery room. PUT YOUR
FEET UP IN THE STIRRUPS. I put them up, obedient,
still humbled, though the spirit was growing larger
in me, that black woman was in my throat, her thin
song, high pitched like a lark, and all the muscles
were starting to constrict around her.
I tried to push just a little. It
didn't hurt. I tried a little more.

ROLL UP, guzzo said. He wanted to give me
a spinal. NO. I DON'T WANT A SPINAL. (same
doctor as axe handle up my butt, same as shaft
of split wood, doctor spike, driving the
head home where my soft animal cowed and prayed and
cried for his mother.)

Or was the baby
part of this
whole damn
conspiracy,
in on it with
guzzo,
the two of them
wanting to shoot
the wood
up me for

nothing,
for playing
music to him
in the dark
for singing
to my round
clasped belly
for filling
up with
pizza on a cold
night, dough
warm.

maybe
he
wanted
out,
was saying

give her
a needle
and let me/the hell/
out of here
who cares
what she
wants
put her
to sleep.

(my baby
pushing off
with his black
feet
from the dark
shore, heading
out, not
knowing
which way and trusting,
oarless and eyeless, so
hopeless
it didn't matter.)

no. not
my baby.
this
loved
thing
in/and of
myself

so i balled up
and let him
try to
stick it in.
    maybe
something was
wrong

Side Effects

ROLL UP
he said
　　ROLL UP
but i don't want it
　　　ROLL UP ROLL UP
but it doesn't hurt

we all stood,
nurses, round the white
light
hands
hanging
empty at our sides
　　　ROLL UP IN A BALL
all of us not
knowing
how
or if
in such a world without
false promises
we could say
anything
but, *yes,*
yes.
come take it
and be quick.

i put my belly in my hand

gave him that
thin side
of my back
the bones
intruding on the air
in little knobs
in joints
he might
crack
down my spine
his knuckles
rap
each twisted
symmetry
put me on
the rack
each
nerve
bright
and stretched
like canvas.

In this plaintive, soul-wrenching poem, the adverse effects of
a medical intervention ramify deeply enough to threaten even
the sacred relationship between mother and her unborn child.
The coercive force of the doctor's order of an epidural block, an
invasive treatment for presumed labor pain (though the young
woman does not even report pain, protesting that "it/didn't

hurt"), leads to the shocking moment of self-questioning when Derricotte becomes alienated from her own infant. Perhaps even more dangerous than nonprogressing labor, one of the common side effects of epidural anesthesia during birth, this profound estrangement between mother and newborn is an extreme exaggeration of the sense expectant mothers report of their fetuses as "foreign bodies." The feminist-inspired movement to demedicalize childbirth is a response to this kind of paradoxical situation, when maternal pain and fear caused by an unnecessary procedure exceed the symptom it is supposed to be alleviating, and may themselves in turn contribute to untoward outcomes.

"ROLL UP" is the gruff command, falling on her repeatedly like so many blows, despite her loud-and-clear statement at the beginning of the poem, "NO. I DON'T WANT A SPINAL." Derricotte likens the experience to rape; the pain of her previous violation by the same doctor, described as an "axe handle up my butt, same as shaft/of split wood," predicts what she goes on to experience as later he tries to get the needle in. "i put my belly in my hand," her protective gesture toward her imperiled baby, can barely precede the drawn-out, literally excruciating lines that describe the botched stabs into her exposed spine; here, the imagery shifts from assault to torture, with "each twisted/symme-try/put me on/the rack," inflicted by the demonic, disembodied, voice-from-below "guzzo." Derricotte renders with searing accuracy not just the humiliation of this ordeal—perhaps the most damaging of all this misguided treatment's side effects—but also its backbreaking, breath-stealing brutality.

A sense of the punitive nature of these adverse effects of treatment is heightened not only by the questionable indication for the use of an epidural block but also by Derricotte's disenfranchised status (made clear in earlier poems in the book) as an unwed black teenage mother. She seems to represent her "otherness" by her dispensing with standard punctuation and capitalization. The poet is at the mercy of the white world of the hospital, populated by white doctors and nurses in their white coats scurrying beneath white lights. Yet somehow she is able to preserve some of herself in this colorless world of erasure; she conceives of birthing as an inherently dark process, "my baby/pushing off/with his black/feet/from the dark/shore." Her affirmation of blackness here is not, however, a retreat into a defended, particularized, angry identity; rather, embedded in the ultimately joyous and universal process of childbirth itself, it seems more of a gesture toward mutual understanding. As we have seen some of the other poets do, through her own poetry she forges empathy out of adversity; rather than a multimillion-dollar malpractice suit (yet another of our disdainfully divisive postmodern inventions), Derricotte seeks a more meaningful and valuable kind of resolution to what was done to her.

In the epiphany at this section of the poem's conclusion, she writes "each/nerve/bright/and stretched/like canvas"—a clear sign that she is not just surviving but transcending the attacks on her identity. Like natural endorphins flooding her with relief, her words become almost visionary, painterly—reintroducing the possibility of color—blacks and browns and reds (the earth tones of the birth itself) to be splashed on her consciousness at the moment of her son's arrival. She invites us into her experience so that we may learn from our mistakes. Art, again, is invoked as a kind of salve. To hear Derricotte read from this poem aloud—she actually sings it in her beautiful, ethereal voice, piercing the listener as pointedly as a needle in the spine, but with an entirely different effect, transforming pain into ecstasy—confirms that her language's beauty heals the anguish it has also conveyed.

Medications themselves also frequently cause side effects, perhaps even more often than procedures such as the one forced on Derricotte. Rika Lesser, a prominent translator of German and Swedish literature, has published three collections of original poetry; her second collection, *All We Need of Hell*, which appeared in 1995, is a gripping pathography of her experiences living with manic-depressive illness, and particularly her difficulties in finding appropriate treatment, and then later the even more disabling side effects she came to suffer from the various medications she was prescribed—as in her poem "On Lithium."

On Lithium

THE THIRD YEAR

I was poisoned, *intoxicated*
a medical text would say, picking
mushrooms in the Swedish woods one day,
late September 1988.
Black ones were scarce; we searched, we scoured.

The Healing Art

When a carpet of trumpets with flame-
yellow stems sounded off, Suzanne knelt,
bobbed, gathered dextrously, while each
time I bent down I grew dizzy. Damned
low blood pressure, I thought. Rooted in
marshy soil, I watched her vacuum two
kilos in no time, barely helped tote
the bags to the car. We'd had a late
start and perhaps three cups of coffee
between our breakfast and our picnic lunch.
(We hadn't been *sampling* the mushrooms,
and we'd shared dinner the night before.)
De-hy-dra-tion, I stammered, stumbling
out of the car. Who thinks about sweat
or thirst when it's fifty degrees? Once
I'd surmised my lithium level
(not my mood) had swung up to a peak,
far from home and shrink, in the coming
weeks I swigged tanks of water each day.

Blood tests in New York confirmed the self-
diagnosis: high time to lower
the dosage. But why, after two years,
suddenly, why?—Don't know, said my shrink,
not contesting the notion that I
now had come home at last. Three months back,
returned from a trip, I'd felt my old
—not my former—self. (We all have

traits we're glad to leave behind.) Jetlagged,
my body had caught up with my mind.

On two capsules daily both my thirst and
hand tremor vanished. My hair hasn't
filled in, the scalp bumps diminished by
vile-smelling selenium and tar
shampoos (recommended by Goran
and Matthew); a Persian rug covers
a patch of oak parquet. It seems I've
adapted.
   —Maybe someday I can
do without lithium carbonate?

—We'll see about that. Why tempt fate?

Home, evidently, is not home free.

Does this still grate? I write with music,
have no visions of infants crawling
on rug or floor . . . Twice resurrected,
once detoxified, now delivered
from a mushrooming fear of illness
(my own as well as my mother's) I'd
say it's clear: that part of myself worth
celebrating came to life this year.

Perhaps most striking about this poem is its subtle tonal shift,
which might be said to represent, first, the poet's mind clouded

by side effects from lithium (a medication commonly used to treat bipolar illness, and one for which it is notoriously difficult to gauge the correct dose for each patient), and then the "detoxified" imagination of the last section. The first two-thirds of the poem have a wooden, somewhat distant, almost dysphoric sound, all the more noticeable in its contrast with the bucolic setting the lines describe, as if the text were experiencing in its slightly stilted diction and off-kilter line breaks the toxicity of a lithium overdose. The last part of the poem, where Lesser describes feeling well, has an easier musical quality, full of pleasing internal rhyme, in bright contrast to the denser previous stanzas. The more concrete imagery of the first part of the poem, which bluntly suggests a comparison between medication and poisonous mushrooms, gives way to the more supple, if not quite playful, punning of the last section (e.g., "a mushrooming fear of illness"). Ultimately, the poem succeeds in integrating these two opposing selves—the well-compensated writer and the overmedicated patient. In reversing the self's undoing through side effects, the struggle over which is so physically manifest in the poet's lines, Lesser kindles empathy in her reader's soul.

Even when showing us the dulling influence of the drug's side effects, however, Lesser is too sentient a poet to allow much to escape her notice. The first line of the poem immediately posits a charged duality between the authentic experience of illness and the doctor's eagerness to rewrite it: "I was poisoned, *intoxicated*/a medical text would say." She is also able to discern irony as she wryly remarks, "Once/I'd surmised my lithium level/(not my mood) had swung up to a peak"—no, it is not her mood that needs treatment (which she seems to believe is the implicit assumption of her "shrink"), it is the treatment that needs to be treated, and in her nonmanic yet drug-impaired state, she is forced to be her own psychopharmacologist. As in Derricotte's poem, the adverse reaction actually serves the attempt to elevate medicine's narrative over the patient's, as the mind-numbing effects of the excess medication threaten to prevent her from writing, and thus from reaching her own conclusions. "*De-hy-dra-tion*, I stammered" seems emblematic of her determination to express herself over the lithium level surging too high in her blood.

Yet the poem does go on to articulate, with remarkable lucidity, not only a veritable catalogue (of practical value) of the side effects of lithium but also a coming to terms with them that again demonstrates poetry's utility in coping with illness. Lesser's precision with language is not at all surprising given that she is such an accomplished translator; but it eloquently refutes popular notions about bipolar patients being "out of control." The act of poem-making itself is thus evidence of her having overcome her illness (and the stereotypes of it) *and* the side effects of its treatment. When she wonders, "—Maybe someday I can/do without lithium carbonate?//—We'll see about that. Why tempt fate?" she is at her lyrical, gut-wrenching best, using all the resources of her art to make sense of her treatment, to make it tolerable, at once questioning the need for it, experiencing its effectiveness, and willing its side effects away. Rhyming "lithium carbonate" and "fate" is not resignation but resolution; isolating the critical second line into its own stanza is a dramatic way of giving pause appropriate to the weight of her realization. The poet, in the end, transcends side effects, and thus recovers for us the primary purpose of any attempt to treat illness: to be made, once again, intelligible to oneself and the world.

X

End of Life

At every station of the disease experience we have examined thus far, poetry has suggested an ulterior discourse that, as it accumulates, forms a composite picture of a humane idea of wellness. Yet when symptoms grow relentless, when the diagnosis seems irrelevant, when treatments no longer work, and when side effects are washed away in the tide of imminent death, one might assume that the heartbeat of poetry would also cease, as if wellness or healing somehow disallowed our mortality. On the contrary, it is here at the threshold of death, where all our costly technologies and toxic medicines have failed in the unbendable quest to cure, that poetry must rise to the occasion. It is now, when our voices seem caught in our throats, that poetry has perhaps its greatest and most unrivaled relevance. Not only does poetry still function in its obvious and familiar guises as prayer and elegy—churches and cemeteries being about the only places one expects to hear poetry in the year 2003—but in the hospice and at the bedside it is also a balm, a potent antidote to the notions of defeat and loss that have so alienated us from the perfectly natural process of dying.

In its sheer durability, poetry is perhaps all the more indispensable at the moment of death. The written word is immortal—all the more truly so nowadays with the advent of indestructible CDs and inexhaustible Internet web sites—and the poems written by the dying can console those who survive them for years to come. Like photographs or heirlooms, they can even introduce the departed to family members yet to be born. In this way, poetry can be imagined to defy death, in the metaphysical sense the work of William Shakespeare and George Herbert exemplifies. These and other poets of premodern times had access to none of the (sometimes thoughtlessly, sometimes cruelly) life-prolonging interventions that have bred the current collective anxiety about dying. Yet for all its wondrous power, I do not believe poetry circumvents mortality; it only humanizes it, by subjecting it to the incontrovertible arguments of breath, voice, and community, by celebrating it though it may cause us pain, by honoring it though it may humble us. All of us survive when poetry does.

In the following poem by Thom Gunn, the question of our survival in the face of epidemic death is taken up with wisdom and courage. Born in England but a resident of San Francisco since the 1950s, Gunn published his *Collected Poems* to exuberant critical acclaim in 1994. His collection *The Man with Night Sweats* was published in 1992, and helped put a human face on the terrible destruction wrought by the AIDS epidemic. He is a winner of the fabled MacArthur "genius" award and Academy

of American Poets Lenore Marshall Poetry Prize. "The J Car" is
reproduced from *The Man with Night Sweats*.

The J Car

Last year I used to ride the J CHURCH Line,
Climbing between small yards recessed with vine
—Their ordered privacy, their plots of flowers
Like blameless lives we might imagine ours.
Most trees were cut back, but some brushed the car
Before it swung round to the street once more
On which I rolled out almost to the end,
To 29th Street, calling for my friend.
        He'd be there, smiling but gaunt,
To set out for the German restaurant.
There, since his sight was tattered now, I would
First read the menu out. He liked the food
In which a sourness and dark richness meet
For conflict without taste of a defeat,
As in the sauerbraten. What he ate
I hoped would help him to put on some weight,
But though the crusted pancakes might attract
They did so more as concept than in fact,
And I'd eat his dessert before we both
Rose from the neat arrangement of the cloth,
Where the connection between life and food
Had briefly seemed so obvious if so crude.

Our conversation circumspectly cheerful,
We had sat here like children good but fearful
Who think if they behave everything might
Still against likelihood come out all right.
    But it would not, and we could not stay here:
Finishing up the Optimator beer
I walked him home through the suburban cool
By dimming shape of church and Catholic school,
Only a few white teenagers about.
After the four blocks he would be tired out.
I'd leave him to the feverish sleep ahead,
Myself to ride through darkened yards instead
Back to my health. Of course I simplify.
Of course. It tears me still that he should die
As only an apprentice to his trade,
The ultimate engagements not yet made.
His gifts had been withdrawing one by one
Even before their usefulness was done:
This optic nerve would never be relit;
The other flickered, soon to be with it.
Unready, disappointed, unachieved,
He knew he would not write the much-conceived,
Much-hoped-for work now, nor yet help create
A love he might in full reciprocate.

Metrical construction and rhyme have the gripping effect of
animating the poem with the body's natural rhythms; this poem's
pulse is lent particular urgency by the poet's friend's impending

death, as though he were so emaciated we can hear his heart beating from across the table. The poet figuratively locates himself in this visit to his friend at the end of life, taking the streetcar that "rolls out almost to the end," yet the verb tense of the line "We had sat here like children good but fearful" raises the possibility the friend has in fact already died. The poem thus straddles the border between the quotidian and the elegiac, insistently calling our attention to the sublime in the mundane. Of course, the poet quickly becomes conscious of his own mortality: there is first the paradise lost of "Climbing between small yards recessed with vine/—Their ordered privacy, their plots of flowers/Like blameless lives we might imagine ours." Then later, as he accompanies his friend back home after their quiet meal, he has the further realization of their precarious connection in "I walked him home through the suburban cool/By dimming shape of church and Catholic school," an intensely evocative couplet that seems a perfect condensation of an ebbing life, as the formerly vibrant physical world now actually recedes, as if shying away from death's nearness—perhaps the two share a Catholic upbringing or education which has taught both fear of the physical body's decay, and also hope in the prospect of salvation. The couplets themselves seem to join the poet over and over again to his friend's fate; that the couplet traditionally appears in love poetry only deepens this boundedness.

Perhaps more salient in Gunn's poem than others' is the clearly nourishing identification with a larger community through illness, so important in much of the writing that has responded to AIDS. The poet must actually "read the menu out" for his sight-impaired friend; similarly, he is obligated to write about his friend's illness. The friend's blindness itself becomes a metaphor for the invisibility of his experience of living with AIDS, pushed unseen to the margins, and literally now to the end of life. His poor appetite, a frequent harbinger of decline in people with advanced HIV infection, is implied in his inability to finish the potato pancakes, or to partake in dessert at all; we infer he wants to eat (and thus to survive), but he cannot. The meal they share, though it does not keep his friend alive, becomes a final ritual of almost religious or spiritual proportions, as suggested by the phrase "the neat arrangement of the cloth," one which brings to mind all the rich symbolism of the Last Supper, with Christ shunned and betrayed, with its bittersweet promise of eternal life through death. "[T]he connection between life and food/Had briefly seemed so obvious if so crude," arresting in its plainspokenness, is dramatized in the poet's finally eating his friend's dessert, a futile effort to sustain his own life and to feel pleasure through what we know will be the inevitable loss—an act that, ironically, only further implicates the poet in human impermanence. The poem creates a luminous space for grieving, and in the meal's consumption the reader in turn feels in the pit of his own stomach the awful unfulfillment of a life cut short by illness, a tremendous sadness, or even an existential loneliness, that is developed further by the colorless anonymity of the phrase "Only a few white teenagers about." The suggestion of a low white blood cell count, the cause of compromised immune function in people with AIDS, seems in keeping with this depleted world.

A burgeoning sense of empathy is created out of the particular details about the dying friend—a young man who (not unlike the medical intern that I was, at the threshold of a career, when I first began thinking about this poem, after reading it in a book a patient with AIDS gave to me) has his own talents and trade, and the untested capacity for love, none of which in this case will reach fruition. The chastened understatement of the entire poem is a metaphor itself for this aching disappointment, muted (but never silenced) by what stands in starkly ironic contrast as the insatiable and omnipresent pandemic. Yet Gunn's ambiguous relationship with his friend, expressed in his stunning last couplet, leaves us at the end of the poem with a redeeming prospect: even if they were not lovers, then it is possible to survive a friend with the same life-affirming intensity of feeling that, when pooled with so many other similar experiences of loss, becomes a well of hope that seems to have been the salvation of the gay community in San Francisco and elsewhere in America. In the most personal of political movements, in a marginalized and scorned community, friends and strangers came together, working tirelessly to mobilize resources and to educate others. ". . . [N]or help create/A love he might in full reciprocate," rather than a jaundiced, blinding defeat, becomes a rallying cry for an entire community; the friend's death *does* help create an ethic of love and mutual respect that has led to changed behaviors, the saving of countless other lives, and increased visibility and tolerance of gay people in society at large.

Like Gunn's work, the writings of poet and memoirist Mark Doty have been central to increasing awareness of AIDS in the

United States. However, in "Bill's Story," the next poem for discussion, the speaker addresses himself to the end of a sister's life from a disease he does not name. Mark Doty was born in 1953. He is the author of five books of poems, including *Atlantis* (1995), which received the Ambassador Book Award and a Lambda Literary Award, and *My Alexandria* (1993), chosen for the National Poetry Series, which won the National Book Critics Circle Award and Britain's T. S. Eliot Prize, and was also a National Book Award finalist. He has received fellowships from the Guggenheim, Ingram Merrill, Rockefeller, and Whiting Foundations, and from the National Endowment for the Arts.

Bill's Story

When my sister came back from Africa
we didn't know at first how everything
had changed. After a while Annie
bought men's and boy's clothes in all sizes,
and filled her closets with little
and huge things she could never wear.

Then she took to buying out
theatrical shops, rental places on the skids,
sweeping in and saying, *I'll take everything.*
Dementia was the first sign of something
we didn't even have a name for,
in 1978. She was just becoming stranger

—all those clothes, the way she'd dress me up
when I came to visit. It was like we could go back
to playing together again, and get it right.
She was a performance artist, and she did
her best work then, taking the clothes to the clubs,
talking, putting them all on, talking.

It was years before she was in the hospital,
and my mother needed something
to hold onto, some way to be helpful.
so she read a book called *Deathing*
(a cheap, ugly verb if I ever heard one)
and took its advice to heart;

she'd sit by the bed and say, *Annie,*
look for the light, look for the light.
It was plain that Anne did not wish
to be distracted by these instructions;
she came to, though she was nearly gone then,
and looked at our mother with what was almost certainly

annoyance. *It's a white light,*
Mom said, and this struck me
as incredibly presumptuous, as if the light
we'd all go into would be just the same.
Maybe she wanted to give herself up
to indigo, or red. If we can barely even speak

to each other, living so separately,
how can we all die the same?
I used to take the train to the hospital,
and sometimes the only empty seats
would be the ones that face backwards.
I'd sit there and watch where I'd been

waver and blur out, and finally
I liked it, seeing what you've left
get more beautiful, less specific.
Maybe her light was all that gabardine
and flannel, khaki and navy
and silks and stripes. If you take everything,

you've got to let everything go. Dying
must take more attention than I ever imagined.
Just when she'd compose herself
and seem fixed on the work before her,
Mother would fret, trying to help her
just one more time: *Look for the light,*

until I took her arm
and told her wherever I was in the world
I would come back, no matter how difficult
it was to reach her, if I heard her calling.
Shut up, mother, I said, and Annie died.

Remarkably, in Doty's moving, precisely worded poem, the
precise diagnosis that causes death is never disclosed to the

reader. Though the possibility of AIDS is present, suggested by the illness's probable origin in Africa, the dementia it causes, and the implication that after 1978 it did have a name (AIDS was not recognized as a specific disease entity until the early 1980s), Doty deliberately chooses to keep it a mystery. In doing so, he focuses on the emotional and spiritual underpinnings of the death experience, rather than its pathologies. "Dying/must take more attention then I ever imagined," he says toward the poem's conclusion, as if to mention the diagnosis itself were too much of a distraction—a sharp comment on modern medicine's clamorous prioritizing of diagnosis and treatment to the neglect of a pure and dignified death. The point is that no matter what, Annie is dying, and she deserves a good death; all else pales in comparison. By refusing us the satisfaction of knowing the cause of her passing, the poet reflects back to us how far we have strayed from what is essential at this juncture in the illness experience: not what Annie is leaving behind, which includes her diagnosis, but rather what lies ahead for us and for her. Reinforcing these observations is the poem's title: at first we have no idea who Bill is, and in the end his specific identity as anyone other than Annie's brother hardly seems important after all; it's important only that her death has become part of his life, his "story," owned by him in a way quite opposite to our usual distancing from our mortality.

Doty is intent on representing death as it truly is, liberated from all the trappings of both superstition and rationalization, the extremes of humanity's unexamined responses to it. If medicine seeks to explain away death, then Bill and Annie's mother wishes to exorcise it in her own way. Doty rejects this way of thinking about death too, dismissing it for its crass devaluing of the experience. The poet knows that death, like every other step in an illness, is not "one size fits all" (recalling Maxine Kumin's incisive response to the generic physiotherapy prescribed for her chronic pain); its universality does not equate with *Chicken Soup for the Soul* glibness. Even the dying Annie resists the "white light" preached at her by her mother, and she comes to, "though she was nearly gone then,/and looked at our mother with what was almost certainly//annoyance." In fact, Annie can only rest in peace once the speaker orders their mother to *"Shut up."* Doty seems to be underscoring that the absence of voice ("voice" as metaphor for self-expression—not merely speech itself) is the defining characteristic of death, a poetic definition more meaningful perhaps than all the complex scientific criteria regarding brain wave activity and cardiac output; not coinciden-tally, the poem also shuts down in the quiet when Annie finally dies.

There are other telltale absences in this masterful poem. Most notable, perhaps, is that no doctors are present at this death, which underscores both the failure of biomedicine to prevent death and also its aversion to enabling or assisting in the death with dignity the speaker so desperately wants for his sister. (Per-haps the invisible doctors have acceded to what we might imag-ine as the mother's request for privacy—as if death should occur behind closed doors, were something to be ashamed of, too awful for the sensitive eyes of others, in keeping with some of her other equally wrongheaded notions—in any event, it does seem significant that no medical provider, not even a nurse or an orderly, witnesses Annie succumb.) The poet is also able to fashion an ineluctable presence by creating another absence: the last stanza of the poem contains only five lines, as compared to all the preceding stanzas' six, as if the last line had been forgotten, or omitted. This missing, unspoken line, all the more eloquent and meaningful in its loss, seems to represent that unknowable moment when death actually takes Annie away from the world of the poem, and figuratively doubles as an acknowledgment of her foreshortened life.

The genuine empathic moment comes earlier in the poem, when the speaker explicitly contemplates death while riding on the train on his way to visit his sister: ". . . sometimes the only empty seats/would be the ones that face backwards./I'd sit there and watch where I'd been//waver and blur out, and finally/I liked it, seeing what you've left/get more beautiful, less specific," he observes (after appreciating the irony in his mother's obtuse belief that we all die the same, though we are barely able to speak to each other in life). Doty ingeniously allows his speaker to enter into death metaphorically: his riding the train facing backwards creates an uncanny sense of both its swiftness and weird gravitational pull, as though drawing us back into ourselves, through our own memories "flashing before our eyes," as we have so often heard said; he finds solace for all of us in what he learns, feeling the pleasure of just letting go, of seeing where he has just been blur into insignificance. In the same way, he seems to say that life's petty concerns quickly dissolve in the beauty of dying. Life slides fluidly, effortlessly, gorgeously

into death, quite literally part of Bill's (and everyone's) jour-
ney—after all, he is on his way to visit Annie. So while death
remains a specific and inevitable terminus for this remarkable
trip, it also is an occasion for universal catharsis, a spiritual
cleansing of the type Aristotle describes in his famous defense of
tragic poetry.

Death's great gift is that it reminds us our little lives must give
us pleasure as we live them—like the pleasure we feel in reading
Doty's poem, heightened by its serious theme, or the speaker's
pleasure in feeling again all the textures of Annie's costumes
even as her condition deteriorates. Despite the awful simulated
life hospitals can orchestrate for us in almost infinite varieties of
medical intervention, the inevitability of death teaches that we
do share deeper biological processes from which we can never
be totally alienated; dying is an opportunity for each to be free
of what mires us in this purgatory of endotracheal intubations
and defibrillations, unnecessary possessions and dysfunctional
families. Annie, suffocating under the piles of unneeded objects
she buys, represents in her affliction these unfortunate aspects of
our postmillennial selves, while her mother, implacably quoting
psychobabble to her on her deathbed, reflects yet another
dimension of our desperate yet misplaced need for meaning.
But it is finally in her death that Annie's family finds a true and
unqualified connection with one another. Expressed in her
brother taking hold of her arm, as if to make more central the
direct, inimitable, delicious power of human touch, of skin on
skin, death becomes palpably each of ours to grasp. Poetry
becomes touch, a creation of the human mind that simply com-

forts rather than strains to explicate. In the poet's promise to search "no matter how difficult/it was" should ever he hear her call—communicated to Annie soundlessly, through his touch itself, in lines of dialogue that notably lack quotation marks—he pledges himself to the most human labor of all, that of quietly fathoming our mortality.

X I

"Eduardo"

duardo started speaking to me in English as I welcomed
him into my exam room that late spring day, which was
odd because we'd always conducted our discussions in
Spanish at his semiannual visits. I noticed his English was halt-
ing and too formal, like the way my grandparents had spoken
it; I assumed he had learned his second language relatively later
in life, as they had. This linguistic rigidity would soon prove
portentous. Eduardo was seventy-six years old and, except for
mild hypertension and diabetes, was remarkably well preserved.
He wore his thick black hair combed back with a strong-
smelling pomade, and in his suit jacket's pocket a handkerchief
folded as precisely as an origami figure declared his fastidious-
ness. He told me he was once a promising young writer in his
native Ecuador, but unmentionable circumstances had forced
him to leave the country, and when he arrived in America he
could only find work as a bellhop at an upscale hotel. He had
stayed in the same job for forty years; it had been backbreaking
work, leaving precious little time, he always said, for cultivating

one's mind. Now that he had finally retired, he vowed that would change.

"Eduardo," I said to him in Spanish, "it's Dr. Campo, remember? We can talk in *castellano*." I expected the flash of his smile, the perfect white teeth that I learned were actually dentures when, to my surprise, he popped them out into his cupped palm in a smooth, single-handed motion the day I first examined him; instead he stared at me vaguely, as though I were speaking in tongues.

I didn't make anything then of the faint tremor in his right arm. In another moment or two, he became his usual loquacious self again, telling me all about his beloved granddaughter's recent piano recital. Out of his wallet came the latest picture of her, her pigtails tied in pink ribbons, her smile brilliant as his, the flash of the camera reflected in one side of the shiny black piano against which she stood. He then segued to his grand plans to tour Spain, where he would visit the haunts of Federico García Lorca, Salvador Dalí, and other members of the avant-garde who were the heroes of his youth. After a check of his blood pressure and a few marks on a lab requisition, I sent him on his merry way.

In the ensuing few months, I diagnosed Eduardo with Parkinson's disease, which progressed so rapidly that he never made his trip to Spain. He fell in his apartment while preparing his supper a few weeks later; unable to take the pot off the stove, the burning *arroz con pollo* was what may have saved his life, by setting off the fire alarms in the building. The paramedics found him prostrated beneath the table in his kitchen, his left hip broken, his neck bleeding, gashed where the knife he'd been using happened to strike him as he crumpled to the floor. As they wheeled him out on a stretcher, he must have asked them to bring along his writing materials; perhaps he had been in the middle of composing a poem, taking a fateful break to slice some tomato for his salad while the rice simmered.

He had pen in hand when I strode in to see him in the hospital the morning after the accident. Now I recognized that the blank stare was not so much disorientation as one of the subtler signs of Parkinson's disease, which robs those it afflicts of most facial expression. A fat wad of gauze was taped to his neck. "Do you like my new friend?" he asked, referring to it with a downward motion of his chin. "It's like a second head, only it has no brain." With that, he mustered a broad smile, displaying his fine false teeth. But it soon vanished again.

When he left the hospital for rehab, after a taxing two weeks of surgery complicated by post-op pneumonia, he presented me with a small packet of poems. They were difficult for me to decipher, line after line of tiny, shaky cursive in Spanish. Because the ink was blotched and uneven, I guessed he had used a fountain pen to write them. It was the first time he had ever shared his work with me, prompted, surely, by his sudden clash with infirmity.

He asked me what I thought of his poetry when he returned to see me in the clinic. I was not especially inclined toward literary critique that day; he'd weathered a prolonged rehabilitation that had been hampered by a further steep decline in his neurological condition, and there was much new data to review.

By now, almost four months later, his gait had become a slow shuffle; his head CT showed the possibility of multiple small basal ganglia infarcts that the neurologist thought might explain his dramatic deterioration. His forgetfulness had also worsened, to the point where when I asked about his granddaughter, whether she had played any new pieces for him, he said he couldn't remember that he even had a granddaughter.

Yet the poems, those he could remember. In fact, he told me he had set himself the task of memorizing them, to combat what he called "the stealing of my personhood." I wasn't sure whether he meant by that the disease itself, or the sedatives that were used to calm his agitation in the evenings—a common phenomenon called "sundowning" in medicalese (and a good if rare example of a medical term for something awful that tries to make it sound somewhat poetic). I sat dumbfounded as he went on to recite about a hundred lines of his verse, the tears coming to his eyes as he described, in one particularly moving section, his granddaughter at the piano, the same talented little girl who earlier during our visit he hadn't been able to recall. His words rose and fell with all the musicality of a concerto by Beethoven or Bach, as if her inerasable presence in his mind had found a last remaining outlet. I wondered whether he had indeed once published his work, in the homeland he could no longer name, in a world that he was fast losing.

Eduardo began to create poems that seemed to be attempts to graft himself back onto the life he once knew. He showed them to me when he came to his appointments, now accompanied by his new attendant, a jovial, buxom, copper-haired Haitian woman named Antoinette. He wrote a poem about what he liked to buy at the supermarket; another recorded the names of the streets in his neighborhood; still another, the names and relationship to him of various family members. There was even a love poem for Antoinette, which made her blush when he read it aloud, though I was quite sure she didn't understand Spanish. I was struck by how their language flowed so effortlessly, no matter how mundane their subjects, animating his face again with the emotions he otherwise could no longer manifest; I noticed how they recollected information, much of it practically useful, some of it simply pleasing, that his faulty neurons could no longer store.

A few months more passed; another springtime in Boston arrived, the golden daffodils like trumpeters heralding a dainty queen's imminent visit. Eduardo failed to keep his morning appointment one day; the inevitable phone call came the same afternoon, from Antoinette. "Don Eduardo, he die," she reported tearfully. She said she had found him utterly motionless in his bed when she'd come to bring him for his appointment; she had recognized immediately the stiffness in his limbs when she tried to rouse him was very different from that caused by Parkinson's disease—"No medicine help him now," is how she put it. I thanked her for taking such good care of him. After a few moments of silence, she told me she found something he had left in his apartment for me, and that she would bring it to the clinic for me the next day.

What she brought was a beautifully handmade book of his poems. Pasted on the cardboard cover was an old photograph of a handsome man with thick black hair combed back neatly. His expression was either very serious or a little scared. He sat at a small desk, upon which were assembled some sheets of paper, a stack of books, and a fountain pen with its inkwell; he cocked his head, looking up from his work, as though his concentration had been interrupted. The desk was positioned before a window, through which I thought I could make out a view of distant mountains, and at their feet, a rim of beach and black water. *"Poesia"* was inscribed in a familiar, tremulous hand beneath the photograph.

Later that week, at his funeral, I sat in a pew alone at the back of the church. After the service, I gave the book to a little girl in pigtails, who smiled at me so genuinely I felt as though I'd known her all her life.

XII

Caregivers

U ntil we become ill ourselves, caring for another is the only way to participate in the healing process directly; in the immediacy of the caregiving relationship— bathing someone who is too weak to hold even a sponge, simply warming the cold hand of someone who is very near death—the old metaphors fall away, anxieties about cultural dissonance dissipate. If poetry is anything, it is a similar kind of care for another person, the reader; yet even poetry struggles to make sense of empathy, even as it enacts it. As much as a sickness pertains to the individual it afflicts, as Gunn and Doty so acutely illustrate, it also deeply and often inconsolably affects those in its proximity. Usually these others are care providers, most often family members, as well as nurses and doctors, physical therapists and chaplains, social workers and interpreters, and even orderlies and phlebotomists. Too often an illness extends its reach even further to ravage a whole community; when we think of such global killers as AIDS, famine, and war, all humankind is implicated. With genocide and pandemic all around us, bearing witness to illness becomes as much an expression of being human as suffering and dying.

I have often turned to the next two poems when I have felt despair in the face of all the pain I will never alleviate in this world. Providing care, that most basic of human interactions, is an especially difficult enterprise in our time. Dizzying technological advancement places ever greater demands on physicians, who must be competent to decipher the expanding barrage of data that spews out at us from the machines that obscure our patients from us, and from the proliferating medical journals that crowd out poetry on our night tables and in our libraries. The constraints of so-called managed care (the ugliest oxymoron ever invented) further interpose barriers between doctor and patient, as reimbursement for care provided dwindles, teaching hospitals go under, and more patients are squeezed into less time to keep up with productivity standards (and sometimes physicians' own selfish desire to preserve their incomes). Whether it is to keep a clinic open to the medically indigent, to pay off interest on medical school loans, or to afford the down payment on a vacation home, money seems to have supplanted the other rewards of caring. Even the richness of our multicultural America threatens care as more and more physicians feel burdened by the need for a translator, or reel at the frustration of a foreign cultural belief that disallows a recommended course of action. The newly risen epidemics of cancer and AIDS, rather than posing a galvanizing challenge, instead have sown a sense of futility among most care providers. Applications to medical school have been down, while dot-com millionaires and greedy CEOs were once ascendant. *Why bother?* seems to be the health care system's unimaginative refrain, with so much seemingly against us.

In Marilyn Krysl's poem "Famine Relief," we are treated to a strong rejoinder to this cynical brand of naysaying. A prominent social activist as well as a gifted poet, Krysl has written seven books of poetry, including *Warscape with Lovers,* which won the Cleveland State University Poetry Center Prize, and also volunteered at Mother Teresa's Kalighat Home for the Destitute and Dying in Calcutta.

Famine Relief

Explain, please, this wonder, this
creaturous pleasure,

this ruby of feeling
while I feed another being: tell me why

when Hasina opens her mouth,
it's as though the world in its entirety

opens, the lotus of the Buddha unfolding
its jewel. Veil of skin, draped over

bone: Hasina's fourteen, so thin
she can't walk, sit up,

hold a cup. Eyes a single beam
scanning for food, even when

she's full. She's the mouth
of the soul, open

around hunger, asking
the way a baby, without guile,

is good with greediness
to know the world. To feed another being

is like eating, both of us
filling ourselves

with the certainty that there is,
in us and around us,

kindness so infinite
that we cannot be lonely. Hasina

might have been the one with the spoon,
fleshy, of substantial body,

I the skeleton—but that too would be
wrong. Under the pull of full sun,

at noon, I hear the temple
gong, summoning the faithful,

and in the lull of echo,
the jangle of bells on the women's

ankles. Hasina looks up,
I lift the spoon, balancing the pans

of our scale: ours
is a life of satiety

and hunger, the haves and have nots,
these two conditions

spread through the universe
so that we may know hunger,

so that we may learn
to feed each other. Not perfection

but the lesson, enacted over
and over again: Hasina and I

by chance or quantum design,
chosen to perform this hallowed, ancient

devotion—one the Venus of Willendorf,
each of those many breasts

overflowing, the other Kali
in her starved aspect

shrill around emptiness,
and devouring, devouring.

In Krysl's numinous poem, starvation itself is revised into a joyful call to purification, an occasion for seeing past the insubstantial human body and directly into the shimmering soul; Hasina is so gaunt (". . . so thin/she can't walk, sit up//hold a cup") she is almost translucent, almost reduced to her gossamer spirit, and thus grows all the more beautiful. Again we see laid bare in poetry the complex intersection of biological and cultural forces; in the face of the most profound physiologic deprivation, the delicious mystical sustenance of empathy abounds. "Explain, please, this wonder, this/creaturous pleasure," the poet begins, rapturously, knowing full well that the transcendent joy she feels is inexplicable in strictly scientific or intellectual terms. She allies herself thus with the good-hearted farmers whose hard work prevents more from starving, while she challenges the modern sciences of agriculture and bioengineering (still not smart enough in this day and age to feed all of us, however much thwarted by political corruption) and ironically underscores their insufficiency.

The delirium of the starvation state is further harnessed to serve the poet's theme of wonder and pleasure; there is an irresistible euphoria in this loving encounter that makes us dizzy ourselves to partake of it. Unlike the heroines of eighteenth-century western European narratives that sanitized and even glamorized tuberculosis, which in some ways similarly consumed its victims (indeed, Hasina's wasted state could also be due in part to undiagnosed TB, given its prevalence in her community), Hasina is not refined and made rarefied by her suffering. Krysl's writing instead draws us closer to Hasina's soul and her plight: the girl's misery, and the empathic response in the poet that it elicits, help to decontaminate the unjust world in which we live. Thus even greediness can be good in the world Krysl depicts, as she brilliantly likens Hasina's ravenous hunger to that of a newborn's developing consciousness. As we have seen before in Hacker's and Gunn's poems, the use of couplets seems to augment the feeling of companionship, of mutual care, in this case between these two women who are all the more fundamentally connected by their participation in what the poet names "this hallowed, ancient/devotion."

Even more astonishing is how Krysl so honestly admits what the impoverished and debilitated Hasina can still give to her. She fully recognizes that Hasina bestows on her a deepened knowledge of her own humanity, and she accepts this great gift of miraculous contact with another human soul reverently. "To feed another being," she intones, "//is like eating, both of us/filling ourselves//with the certainty that there is,/in us and around us,//kindness so infinite/that we cannot be lonely." The frail Hasina thus single-handedly delivers the poet from her solitude, and she acknowledges with gratitude how she herself is nourished. Krysl is not a patronizing American do-gooder providing charity to assuage her own guilt; in the act of giving care, she feels her own needs being satisfied as she satisfies the needs of another. In her communion with Hasina, she makes herself vulnerable, genuinely opening herself to the other woman, through which the cultural differences she alludes to in her references to the Venus of Willendorf and Kali are also bridged; the presumptuous phoniness of some politicians' mantra of "I feel your pain" (no matter how well intentioned) could not be more eloquently discredited.

In Krysl's poetic estimation, Hasina is not to be consigned to the faceless and numberless population of dark-skinned people whom the industrialized world is content to let starve; neither is she a tear-jerking stand-in for the latest liberal yet paternalistic cause. Emphatic and unadorned as her "devouring, devouring" at the poem's conclusion, perhaps suggesting godliness in her abjection, in the end she remains no more or less than another human being. She is the specific location of the necessary other half of the empathic gesture of a poem. She cannot be placated or dismissed, and she refuses any facile effort to save her. Rather, by her very existence, she demands our care, she insists on life. The subtle irony of the poem's title, "Famine Relief," is searing in its accuracy: Give us a break, it seems to say, get real. The poem, like Hasina, has no time for oxymoronic euphemisms (as if famine could ever be relieved by the piddling aid programs rich nations extend to those they have exploited for their own benefit); it requires immediate action, of the sort it exemplifies, that floods across national and political borders and penetrates even the defenses of individualistic self-interest. In a world of obscenely wealthy rock stars who cut albums that conveniently give them publicity while marginally helping struggling Iowa farmers or starving Sudanese children, Krysl's poem resounds with its forthright humility and compassion; her plaintive song, as radical as it is old, is itself, in its indisputable invocation of our common humanity, a catalyst for healing.

Miroslav Holub, a Czech citizen who wrote prolifically until his sudden death in 1998, remains likely the most important physician-poet of the current moment. His work is internationally known, and he was frequently short-listed for the Nobel Prize in literature. He was a survivor of both Nazism and later Stalinist Communism. Still, he retained an unsentimental and yet deeply empathic view of the world in which we live, which is reflected in the following poem:

Suffering

Ugly creatures, ugly grunting creatures,
Completely concealed under the point of the needle,
> behind the curve of the Research Task Graph,
Disgusting creatures with foam at the mouth,
> with bristles on their bottoms,
One after the other
They close their pink mouths
They open their pink mouths
They grow pale
Flutter their legs
> as if they were running a very
> long distance.

They close ugly blue eyes.

They open ugly blue eyes
    and
    they're
    dead.

But I ask no questions,
no one asks any questions.

And after their death we let the ugly creatures
    run in pieces along the white expanse
    on the paper electrophore
We let them graze in the greenish blue pool
    of the chromatogram
And in pieces we drive them for a dip
    in alcohol
    and xylol
And the immense eye of the ugly animal god
    watches their every move
    through the tube of the microscope

And the bits of animals are satisfied
like flowers in a flower pot
    like kittens at the bottom of a pond
    like cells before conception.
But I ask no questions,
    no one asks any questions,
Naturally no one asks
Whether these creatures wouldn't have preferred

to live all in one piece,
    their disgusting life
    in bogs
    and canals,
Whether they wouldn't have preferred to eat
    one another alive,
Whether they wouldn't have preferred to make love
    in between horror and hunger,
Whether they wouldn't have preferred to use
    all their eyes and pores to perceive
    their muddy stinking little world
Incredibly terrified,
Incredibly happy
In the way of matter which can do no more.

But I ask no questions,
    no one asks any questions,
Because it's all quite useless,
Experiments succeed and experiments fail,
Like everything else in this world,
    in which the truth advances
    like some splendid silver bulldozer
    in the tumbling darkness,

Like everything else in this world,
    in which I met a lonely girl
    inside a shop selling bridal veils,
In which I met a general covered

with oak leaves,
In which I met ambulance men who could find no
    wounded,
In which I met a man who had lost
    his name,
In which I met a glorious and famous, bronze,
    incredibly terrified rat,
In which I met people who wanted to lay down
        their lives and people who wanted to lay down
        their heads in sorrow,
In which, come to think of it, I keep meeting my
        own self at every step.

In contrast to William Carlos Williams, who made his poems
modern while preserving a distilled humane essence in which
emotion itself became the "thing" observed, Holub trenchantly
subverts the postmodern nightmare of fragmentation and con-
tamination in the service of a more sweeping and even holistic
vision of empathic care. Williams was positioned at the begin-
ning of the modern era, with "magic bullet" antibiotics and
newfangled technologies promising to end human suffering; he
viewed the care relationship with a kind of technocratic hope,
in which on a case-by-case basis he might find idiosyncratically
significant "material for a work of art that made [the patient]
somehow come alive" (as he said in his autobiography, in the
chapter he called "Of Medicine and Poetry"). Krysl and now
Holub seem to report on a place where science not only has
failed us but has perversely contributed to our ailments, which

now require the grand-scale, last-ditch balm of the poem. For the modernist Williams, caring for patients inspired an attempt to isolate pure, unadulterated acts of perception. For these more contemporary poets, pathos must be added back into a care relationship overly determined by false objectivity and sterile methodologies. "Ugly creatures, ugly grunting creatures,/Completely concealed under the point of the needle,/behind the curve of the Research Task Graph," begins Holub's poem, and we are immediately the trivialized victims of our own unfeeling technologies; the ugly creatures are heartlessly dissected down to postmodern "pieces." Instead of elevating us to some diaphanous plane of self-knowledge, science has objectively revealed us to ourselves as hideous, inconsequential, unthinking beings.

This irony is only heightened by the dispassionate refrain of "But I ask no questions,/ no one asks any questions," echoing throughout the tiled laboratory. If science is anything, it is asking a question and then subjecting it to some set of principles by which an answer to the question is sought; yet in this scary cultureless and conscienceless world, with electrophores and chromatograms and xylol all around, no question is ever asked or answered. Hypothesis in Holub's poem thus becomes only a mockery of our humanity. "Experiments succeed and experiments fail," he laments with only half-feigned resignation, standing as he does upon the eastern European rubble of two totalitarian systems that infamously used science to support repression and genocide, and conducted experiments on human subjects against their will, "undesirables" who were later mercilessly killed—much like the hapless "ugly creatures" in the poem.

Holub thus contemplates the worst of all possible worlds: one where science has completely permeated not just the air we breathe and the food we eat but also the very culture by which we understand ourselves. The refrain of the poem haunts us as much as it taunts us; it conjures mass production, the automatic clanking of the assembly line, the nightmare of routinized suffering. Holub warns us that when culture becomes so determined by technologies through which more and more people have their lives hyperrealistically simulated for them, as in TV docudramas and Internet virtual reality games and Hollywood blockbusters and ICUs, even a biocultural model of illness may not permit meaningful, life-sustaining care. Yet even at this nadir of the imagination, Holub does not capitulate to despair. The poem he writes, against our science-laden culture's exhortations, speaks the unspeakable, imagines the unimaginable, and finally proves its mettle as a true medium for examining, and indeed reclaiming, the nature of human suffering. The poem, in the end, exists in spite of all attempts to squelch it.

The abhorrent immorality of the postmodern "isms" Holub survived is most explicitly and brilliantly contradicted by the poem in its moving last stanza. Before the penultimate stanza's "splendid silver bulldozer" of truth, a wonderful image that melds the allure, power, and paradoxical devastation associated with "progress," these concluding lines deploy their vividly depicted characters almost like protesters blocking a road at a rally against injustice. The "ugly creatures" are suddenly seen not with the disfiguring lenses of a microscope or the corrupting distance of a satellite, but by poetry—through which, when individual pain is made clearly visible, the end of entire political systems can be heralded. Even the demoralizing refrain of bankrupt science is no longer heard; gone also are all the disturbing trappings of its soullessness. All of us are reborn as human beings in the culminating lines of the poem, through the restorative power of empathy, as Holub assembles a ragtag, Wizard-of-Oz-like community of the "lonely girl" (like Hasina?) in the bridal veil shop, the ambulance driver who finds no wounded, and the people who want to lay down their lives, or their heads in sorrow—even the awful rat, perhaps a reference to Orwell's *Nineteen Eighty-four*, bronzed and terrified like an old Soviet statue of Lenin about to be razed, has its place among us. The care relationship, the poet-physician at once joyously and ferociously concludes, is one that through poetry demands change on this largest of stages—and one that yet remains intimate, self-realizing, "in which, come to think of it, I keep meeting my/own self at every step."

XIII

Transcendence

It is more than just immortality, but also the triumph of good over evil upon which our survival as a species depends, that poetry must continue to strive to attain. Perhaps poetry, unlike science, is more forgiving of another human capacity, one I have not yet directly addressed, that of enmity—equally a part of us as empathy, and yet often, it seems, the more readily accessible to us. A poem that spews hatred or spreads untruths cannot harm us quite in the same way a nuclear missile aimed at an enemy's city or the smallpox virus released in our subways could; another poem offering an empathic rejoinder can be created more expeditiously than a water supply decontaminated. With our far greater success at killing as compared to healing, imperiling the collective good, one wonders whether humanity is prepared even to consider the prospect of immortality; until we can learn to better harness the awesome power of science, perhaps all we can bear to contemplate is the gentler kind of life everlasting that is possible in poetry. The strange fates of the likes of Ponce de León, who died himself in the paradoxically genocidal pursuit to discover the mythical Fountain of Youth, and Linus Pauling, who tarnished much of his own contribution to scientific advancement with his later bizarre theories about prolonging life, serve as cautionary tales of the inauthentic quest for immortality.

Of course, none of us can live forever. Yet the poem does provide a certain heartening opportunity for immortality that reveals as maladroit many of science's attempts over the centuries to achieve the same elusive goal. Alchemy, cryogenics, cloning, and even the latest stem cell research all seem to tremble beside the timeless wit and wisdom of John Donne's metaphysical sonnets or the enduring beauty of the Navajo night chant. We believe the victims of the terrorist attacks on the World Trade Center and the Pentagon live on forever in the elegies that memorialize them, whether written by schoolchildren or acclaimed poets in their honor; tragically, none of our sophisticated radar systems and intelligence gathering devices were enough to prevent their deaths, and indeed some of those very same technologies surely helped make possible the devastation. Science continues to dream, as it must, sometimes blindly, often hopefully, and always ambitiously; poetry *is* the dream. Maybe, says poetry, we can transcend our tendency to do away with ourselves after all.

Tim Dlugos never won a major award for his poetry before his death in 1990 of complications from AIDS. His life ended before he could gain the kind of recognition that might superficially (through a more banal definition of fame) seem to confer immortality. Yet his poem *"D.O.A.,"* which I reproduce below,

is in my estimation one of the most memorable contemporary
poems written in English:

D.O.A.

"You knew who I was
when I walked in the door.
You thought that I was dead.
Well, I am dead. A man
can walk and talk and even
breathe and still be dead."
Edmond O'Brien is perspiring
and chewing up the scenery
in my favorite film noir,
D.O.A. I can't stop watching,
can't stop relating. When I walked down
Columbus to Endicott last night
to pick up Tor's new novel,
I felt the eyes of every
Puerto Rican teen, crackhead,
yuppie couple focus on my cane
and makeup. "You're dead,"
they seemed to say in chorus.
Somewhere in a dark bar
years ago, I picked up "luminous
poisoning." My eyes glowed
as I sipped my drink. After that,

there was no cure, no turning back.
I had to find out what was gnawing
at my gut. The hardest part's
not even the physical effects:
stumbling like a drunk (Edmond
O'Brien was one of Hollywood's
most active lushes) through
Forties sets, alternating sweats
and fevers, reptilian spots
on face and scalp. It's having
to say goodbye like the scene
where the soundtrack violins go crazy
as O'Brien gives his last embrace
to his girlfriend-*cum*-Girl
Friday, Paula, played by Pamela
Britton. They're filmdom's least
likely lovers—the squat and jowly
alkie and the homely fundamentally
talentless actress who would hit
the height of her fame as the pillhead-
acting landlady on *My Favorite Martian*
fifteen years in the future. I don't have
fifteen years, and neither does Edmond
O'Brien. He has just enough time to tell
Paula how much he loves her, then
drive off in a convertible
for the showdown with his killer.
I'd like to have a showdown too, if I

could figure out which pistol-packing
brilliantined and ruthless villain
in a hound's-tooth overcoat took
my life. Lust, addiction, being
in the wrong place at the wrong
time? That's not the whole
story. Absolute fidelity
to the truth of what I felt, open
to the moment, and in every case
kind of love: all of the above
brought me to this tottering
self-conscious state—pneumonia,
emaciation, grisly cancer,
no future, heart of gold,
passionate engagement with a great
B film, a glorious summer
afternoon in which to pick up
the ripest plum tomatoes of the year
and prosciutto for the feast I'll cook
tonight for the man I love,
phone calls from my friends
and a walk to the park ignoring
stares, to clear my head. A day
like any, like no other. Not so bad
for the dead.

What is so remarkable about this poem is its ability to create
a state of vibrant living despite its author's having already died.

More successfully even than the film from which it borrows its central metaphor, it contains two opposing ideas, generating a miraculous transcendence from their tension. In an extension of the healing willed in so many of the previous poems, we are catapulted even further, toward immortality itself. This state of "luminous poisoning," a metaphorical commingling of life and death forces, makes sense of the incomprehensible through art. Dlugos, now dead, eerily and triumphantly speaks again in the poem's opening lines, quoted from the movie's script. "You thought that I was dead./Well, I am dead. A man/can walk and talk and even/breathe and still be dead," says the poet, inhabiting the voice of another ghost, Edmond O'Brien, long dead himself and yet still capable of inspiring the urgent connection into which we are all immediately drawn. That Dlugos can enter into this dialogue with an obscure and self-destructive Hollywood star who in spite of his human frailties does live forever, is not just another example of the cross-generational communication made possible through art but also a persuasive dramatization of the eternal life to which he lays claim.

As if to refute arguments based on semantic distinctions as to the definition of immortality—that even if his poem in some senses lives, the poet still has died—Dlugos fortifies "*D.O.A.*" with enough physicality and lyricism to make us feel as though he were reincarnated here with us as we read the poem. We feel his intense engagement with the film, the ghostly, luminous screen in a dark room somehow captured in the way he crosses into its world, his eyes glowing when he partakes of the mysterious poison; we experience his disequilibrium as later he shuffles down the street, hobbled by neuropathy, in the awkward, jerking enjambment of the poem's short lines. Ingeniously, he goes on to project himself into the future in his hilarious aside about Pamela Britton, the film's costar, "the homely fundamentally/talentless actress who would hit/the height of her fame as the pillhead-/acting landlady on *My Favorite Martian*/fifteen years in the future."—a complicating reminder of the insignificance of human lives, which only lends a deeper poignancy to his own imminent demise. Just as we see Dlugos outliving Britton, asserting a kind of superiority over her in summing up her career (and mocking her petty mortal accomplishments), he jolts us back into his present moment, reminding us that "I don't have/fifteen years, and neither does Edmond/O'Brien." In this passage, Dlugos further implies that his poem is the more sturdy vehicle for the journey to Elysium; the modern technology that makes film images possible is diminished in comparison to the poet's command of this imaginative space. Time dilates and telescopes three-dimensionally in the weird realm of eternal life made possible in poetry; the flatter black-and-white images of film and television media seem to recede into lesser relevance.

Dlugos is not content to stop here, resplendent with the poet's power to bend time. He then moves into a brilliant fantasy about confronting his killer; another compelling aspect of life everlasting is the opportunity it affords to right wrongs, which Dlugos juxtaposes with the more existential notion that he is in fact his own assassin. Yet redemption for the poet ultimately lies neither in retribution nor in regret. Rather, he buttresses our impression of his enduring presence by citing a list brimming with the immediacy of what he feels and knows: "Absolute fidelity/to the truth of what I felt, open/to the moment, and in every case/a kind of love: all of the above/brought me to this tottering/self-conscious state—pneumonia,/emaciation, grisly cancer,/no future, heart of gold,/passionate engagement with a great/B film, a glorious summer/afternoon in which to pick up/the ripest plum tomatoes of the year/and prosciutto for the feast I'll cook/tonight for the man I love,/phone calls from my friends/and a walk to the park ignoring/stares, to clear my head." At once a ringing manifesto for brave persistence and an honest self-elegy imbued with an appreciation of time's limitedness, Dlugos provides all the ingredients necessary for transcendence. The poem becomes a kind of magic portal through which vital sensuality creates and is satisfied by the bounty of what is culturally manufactured and available on the pulsing streets of New York City (itself a place that is endlessly alive). "A day/like any, like no other. Not so bad/for the dead" completes the paradoxical epiphany of the poem, and this great poet, I know in the deepest places of my soul, lives on.

If part of what allows Dlugos his access to immortality is this paradoxical acceptance of his death—as if it were perfectly usual to be deceased and out doing some errands—then the next poet might seem at first glance to frustrate her own claim to transcendence. But then again, Audre Lorde made her career and her art out of defying expectations. Born in 1932, she was the author of numerous collections of poetry and critical essays which dealt unabashedly with her interpenetrating identities as a black lesbian mother. Breast cancer, which took her life in 1992, only served as another lens through which to examine her most beloved theme, that of social justice. Among her many honors and awards, she was the recipient of a National Book Award for a collection of her later prose, and was named New York State Poet Laureate in 1991.

A Song for Many Movements

Nobody wants to die on the way
caught between ghosts of whiteness
and the real water
none of us wanted to leave
our bones
on the way to salvation
three planets to the left
a century of light years ago
our spices are separate and particular
but our skins sing in complementary keys
at a quarter to eight mean time
we were telling the same stories
over and over and over.

Broken down gods survive
in the crevices and mudpots
of every beleaguered city

where it is obvious
there are too many bodies
to cart to the ovens
or gallows
and our uses have become
more important than our silence
after the fall
too many empty cases
of blood to bury or burn
there will be no body left
to listen
and our labor
has become more important
than our silence.

Our labor has become
more important
than our silence.

Lorde's poem, which was first collected in *The Black Unicorn*, reappears and is given new life in her later book *The Cancer Journals* as part of a preface she called "The Transformation of Silence in Language and Action." Long before the rallying cry of SILENCE = DEATH so effectively promulgated by AIDS activists, Lorde was already envisioning a profound connection between speaking out against injustice and enduring. In her work, the biological disease of cancer was unquestionably an expression of the cultural tribulations of homophobia and racism with which she was forced to contend every day of her thinking life; survival meant battling these oppressive and omnipresent forces. Here is an example of a poet who redefines the militaristic fantasies surrounding illness to serve her needs as a cancer survivor. Far from being hindered by them, she productively harnesses her own rage (and yes, hope) as she assumes the roles of warrior-woman, Amazon, freedom fighter—and most of all, of master poet who threw herself into the fray of body and culture, and who in doing so defied the odds against her (lesbians and blacks have much lower breast cancer survival rates than their heterosexual and white counterparts), and lived for many more years after her diagnosis than was prognosticated.

Lorde thus achieves her transcendence almost in spite of herself; hers is the kind of courage that would lead her to gladly lay her life down for another. Yet she does not go in for strident hollering and seething accusation. Instead she strips her language down to its barest essentials, achieving an elemental idiom we might imagine is spoken in whispers among immortal spirits. Like Dlugos, she presents us with the possibility of having already died: "Nobody wants to die on the way/caught between ghosts of whiteness/and the real water/none of us wanted to leave/our bones/on the way to salvation" begins the poem, with the change of verb tense ever so faintly suggesting that a great loss has transpired; it is not until the sixth line of the poem that we realize that the journey to which she alludes is the ethereal one toward salvation. Just as she dispenses with most punctuation, so does she shed her flesh, in effect becoming the sounds of her words themselves—thus does poetry represent both our physical and spiritual essences. More than that, the poet becomes the instrument of an unending narrative, a chimerical entity that reaches across boundaries of biological race and societal culture (signified in the metaphor-mixing phrases "our spices are separate" and "our skins sing in complementary keys") into the fundamentally empathic circle she enters of "we were telling the same stories/over and over and over." Listening, she contends, is the critical faculty necessary for recovery.

The poet's surprising equanimity soon gives way to quiet outrage as she acknowledges that this life-sustaining empathy is imperiled by its opposite, enmity. From her disembodied vantage point, she becomes a keen witness to some of the starker realities of the postmodern condition. "Broken down gods survive/in the crevices and mudpots/of every beleaguered city," she observes, "where it is obvious/there are too many bodies/to cart to the ovens/or gallows," with searing, almost scriptural concision, recalling some terrible cross between Marilyn Hacker's dystopian New York and Marilyn Krysl's famine-ravaged India. Lorde's view of our world of genocide, near godlessness, and poverty mutely cries out from the dust to be healed even as the symbolic body, Christ-like, is literally consumed: "there will be no body left/to listen," she warns, oracular, above the devastated warscape. While the metaphors she employs are sometimes borrowed and sometimes her own, sometimes fearsome and sometimes ordinary, they all point toward a transcendence that is relevant to everyone. So the work of a doubly marginalized poet who, rather than raging, continues to speak so softly, belies the postmodern notion that there is no longer anything we all have in common.

The simple, almost unremarkable, and yet ingenious repetition of the second stanza's last three lines, which are revived to become the final stanza all to themselves, offers us all a glorious resurrection. Words and poetry become more than gestures toward mere persistence, cultural relics to be dusted off by future readers in a shadowy library; they are actively imagined as agents of change, as physically charged as heavy legs after a civil rights march on Washington or bruised arms raised to deflect a gay basher's blows to the head—or shoulders aching and sore from burying a sister dead of breast cancer. From the rudimentary, the unprettified, the unadorned, the almost elided, the (in the traditional sense) unpoetic, Lorde fashions an entire discourse against oppression. Yet in place of the raucous diatribes on hot-button issues we see on talk shows and in tabloids, her understated lines celebrate instead those more banal aspects of existence—labor, small talk, kindness—that are indelibly catholic indicators of our humanity.

Like Christ himself—poor, marginalized, gentle, plain, and austere—this poet seems an unlikely redeemer of a world so utterly degraded. "Our labor has become/more important/than our silence," she bravely concludes, at once calling us to a better life and enacting change itself in her subtle, almost unnoticeable rearrangement of the lines from how they appeared previously (thus proving herself capable of rewriting the story that is supposed to end in death). It is as if she means that everything depends, to paraphrase William Carlos Williams, on what we might easily overlook. More than an uplifting reaffirmation of a shared struggle against oppression, more than a rejection of those who fail to join in the human work of empathy, Lorde leaves us with a fitting valediction: in poetry, that most valuable effort against the dark, we all just might live and love forever.

XIV

"Ms. Twomey"

When I arrive, she is sitting beside her hospital bed in one of those tall, vinyl-upholstered chairs that looks like it might recline comfortably but actually doesn't. An adjustable tray bearing what might be called lunch is angled before her, as though she has pushed it away; I can see through the translucent plastic covers on the plates that she hasn't touched any of it, not the perfect scoop of mashed potatoes, not the gray-brown square of pot roast, not the pyramid of tiny wrinkled peas. Futuristically geometric food, suitable to the sterile confines of the wards, surroundings as white and airless as what we imagine a spaceship's interior would be like. Faint humming from nowhere and everywhere; sporadic beeps.

"Oh, it's you," she says, and I return from the future. She is wrapped in the standard-issue blue-checkered hospital gown. She looks terribly gaunt. I remember why I've come.

I am trying to understand why I have never liked her, this woman I will call Ms. Twomey. I have been her doctor for more than six years. During that time, surely, the cancers, one in her

179

colon and another in her breast, slowly developed and grew, and maybe even metastasized. I suppose I should admit that when she came to see me last week for a regular follow-up appointment, dressed in her usual prim attire—the same beige cable-knit sweater loosely buttoned over the same cream rayon blouse, and the same calf-length navy blue pleated skirt—I felt something akin to vindication, or even pleasure, as she complained matter-of-factly that she was feeling listless. Her cheap perfume, as on her previous visits, only partially obscured the sour odor of old sweat from beneath her arms.

I knew as soon as she walked in my office that day that she was out of sorts. Though her clothes were neat as ever, I noticed that her white hair was not as carefully groomed as it always was. Her thin lips were a faint bluish color, and she swooned slightly, steadying herself on my arm when she rose for me to check her blood pressure. She had never spontaneously touched me before. When I felt through the sleeve of my shirt how cold her hand was on the back of my arm, I was sure she must be anemic. Given her advanced age—she would be eighty-four in December, just a few weeks away—I guessed even then that it would turn out to be a cancer of some sort. What really surprised me, more than the glimpse of death's visage, was the feeling I had that she deserved it.

Just as she had that day in my office, she sits with her hands folded in her lap, looking impassively ahead so that I am kept in the periphery of her field of vision. "They tell me it's bad," she says. A long pause before she adds, "The cancer." By "they," she is referring to the hospitalist, I think, and the general surgeon, who have been managing her since she was admitted, the day after our last visit. She had indeed turned out to be anemic—hematocrit of 20, to be precise, with a marked microcytosis. The colonoscopy I had arranged urgently, with the help of the clinic social worker, who assisted her with the last-minute transportation, showed a six-centimeter adenocarcinoma in the ascending colon. I can't imagine the indignity of the test for her, she who was too prim and proper to allow me to examine anything more than her blood pressure on her biannual visits; even harder to imagine is the medical student examining her breasts upon her admission to the hospital and finding a mass the size of a baseball. "I should have let you do the mammogram," she says now, resigned if anything, and not particularly regretful. Her hand now clutches absently at the opening of her gown below her neck.

I suppose I should say something comforting to her, but the spiky whiskers on her chin stop me. I never noticed them before; they glisten a little in the sunlight the window lets in. Though I've been in these hospital rooms hundreds of times before, today the windows seem so large, as if to encourage breathing, or even flight. Ms. Twomey's overlooks the women's college's athletic fields across Brookline Avenue, vast green squares, almost pastoral. I notice their manicured appearance reflected in her wide-rimmed glasses, their milky white plastic frames, inexpensive and unfashionable, like the last pair my grandmother wore. Life and order juxtaposed on dissolution and death, I think rather heartlessly; not even the unusual warmth of the late autumn day outside, or the fleeting memory of my own grandmother, is enough to inspire my pity.

It isn't that she routinely refused almost all of the health maintenance interventions I would offer her; it isn't her South Boston Irish accent, either, that I find so distasteful, or even her body odor. I can't put my finger on it. I am not used to being unable to empathize. When I give readings of my poetry, I like to share the story about when I was a young resident, and one of my attendings wrote an evaluation that criticized me for identifying too strongly with my patients. Usually the audience gasps and groans a little when they hear this story. Sometimes tears come again to my eyes when I retell it, because after all these years the cruelty of those words, scrawled hastily on a sheet of yellow lined paper stuffed in a folder with my name on it, still stings.

I am no longer a thin-skinned trainee, though, and I have no attending telling me to be tougher, so why can't I engage with Ms. Twomey on this glorious afternoon? Why can't I reach out and take her hand in mine? Suddenly my mind is flooded with all the obstacles to empathy that I am so fond of reciting, familiarly framed problems for the medical students and residents: the burgeoning technologies of medical science, which place ever more machines between doctors and patients; the constraints of managed care, which puts the interests of the afflicted at odds with those of their caregivers in complex ways; the challenge of our increasingly multicultural society, which too often and too easily allows each to see the other as incomprehensibly alien. True, she had come to diagnosis through the implementation of expensive machines, but none interposed themselves at the moment; even the device that controlled her IV fluid rate was

turned off, its fat, gelatinous bag of saline suspended uncon-
nected to anything, as if sulking in the corner of the room. True,
she had a type of insurance that failed to fully reimburse the
hospital's charges for the care she required, but no utilization
review nurse was knocking to tell us brusquely she must be dis-
charged today. Even the fact of our disparate points of origin
seemed irrelevant; if anything, as children of immigrant parents,
albeit from different generations and different island cultures,
we likely had more in common than most doctors and their
patients. As I stand here in her doorway, feeling intensely how
much I don't want to sit on her bed and stay to chat, this litany
sounds canned, glib.

If I happen to be addressing a medical audience, often a silver-
haired Marcus-Welby-gone-wrong type in the back of the
auditorium will complain that one can't "teach" empathy; it's
either already there somewhere inside a person, he says gruffly,
or it's not. I love this objection, because I can retort that while
it's probably true that empathy can't be grafted onto the unwill-
ing soul, at the very least it can be modeled, and through such
modeling, even the most rudimentary or stunted capacity for
empathy can be nurtured. Bring poems about illness on rounds,
I say cheerfully; embrace a patient after the physical examina-
tion is concluded, remain open to sharing a spontaneous joke.
Make a point of asking for any questions, or greeting family
members who might be present at the bedside. Ask patients to
keep a journal, to share their own poems and stories and small
insights with you. If his beeper hasn't gone off calling him away
to a less philosophical situation—I know he must have a very

sick crew of inpatients, and I actually empathize with *him*, imagining his frustration in dealing with the GI bleeder with alcohol withdrawal seizures in the ICU, or the demented elder who can't safely return home alone but who has repeatedly declined placement in long-term care facilities, or any of countless other commonplace and irremediable scenarios—my interlocutor usually looks exasperated by my answer, as if one more unreasonable demand has just been made of him.

I know I am often dismissed as a daydreamer, an impractical poet, so I often try to support my arguments with references to the likes of the literary theorist Susan Sontag or the social anthropologist David Morris; sometimes I cite political activist poets like Audre Lorde and Adrienne Rich and June Jordan. I distribute a poem by William Carlos Williams I've photocopied. I give examples of how negative metaphors for illness constructed by our culture can color our thinking about our patients, when we talk of blasting tumors with radiation or when we imagine the agony of withdrawal as a kind of punishment for the narcotics addict. I point out how the kind of language patients might use themselves to describe their experiences of illness, more positive and affirming, might fuel a mind-body interaction within them that has healing potential. By now the room is beginning to empty of audience, and the drug rep starts to pack up any leftover sandwiches. They are all returning to the innumerable stories they are helping to construct, barely awakened to their role in those dramas, happier to ignore the untidy cultural fascinations and distortions that so much more than X-ray interpretations or biopsy results define the experience of illness, intent only that the onerous work of the hospital continue.

Ms. Twomey gazes toward the windows; I realize that I have been filling our uncomfortable silence with my ruminations. Then she says it, as though she were addressing one of the large oaks that blaze orange at the far end of the fields. "I am not afraid to die, like you think I am." Her words are punctuated by the distant shouts and laughs of the Simmons field hockey team, which has begun to spill some of life's happy disorder onto the perfect grass: afternoon practice, the thrill and release of being free of the classroom and the library, free of concepts and chalk dust and theories, in the realm of the body, the physical, the pleasure of adrenaline and hard breathing. By the time the young women begin their scrimmage, Ms. Twomey is quietly sobbing.

Several weeks later, I find myself writing again, and I am writing about Ms. Twomey. Her tears seem more than a vivid detail that describes my visit with her that day; now I understand them as a form of language itself, perhaps the only language which can accommodate a true definition of empathy. The poem I write, and now these paragraphs, can only approximate the feeling that joined us at that moment. Indeed, one of the pitfalls of empathy is the kind of paradoxical hubris it can breed, which tempts us to believe that we can truly know and thus explicate the experience of another person's suffering. Yet such is our utterly and fundamentally human limitation, each of us born into families and communities full of their mysteries and contradictions, their pleasures and their pain, human gath-

erings we yearn to join. Equally human, it seems, is our impulse
to transcend that limitation, to attempt to make sense of that
innate need for communion. Whatever the reason I could not
embrace Ms. Twomey that awful day—for shame or guilt, revul-
sion or rage—to tell the story of us, together amidst those tears,
assumes a greater urgency. To see the day declining into a night
as sorely purple-red as a bruise—to know that her injury in
admitting mortality is the same one I must suffer someday—is a
biological drive, a process of living. Here, then, is the reason I
am hopeful; here, in this brief narrative I create, in my poem
that I dedicate to her, in this tether between two people, is the
meaning we all seek in life.

AFTERWORD

Eve

I have tried to show in my discussion of individual poems derived from the experience of illness that there does exist an expressive medium in language capacious enough to make empathy for human suffering, if not entirely comprehensible, then at least clearly and palpably evident. Contrary to the rather cynical dictum promulgated by a vocal minority of postmodernist critics that nothing in human experience is universal, these poems and our responses to them offer an eloquent argument that even across diverse maladies and disparate authorial points of origin, a common propensity toward empathy exists in each one of us. My thesis has been that if the human narrative impulse is indeed biologically determined, then it follows that the empathic response a good narrative engenders in its audience is likewise as universal as the serotonin receptors in our brains, or our very DNA. While there are several fascinating hypotheses that arise from evolutionary biology to explain such phenomena as altruism and empathy, I hope to have shown that it is equally important simply to allow for the mystery of how poetry speaks for itself, and, as we have done here, to immerse ourselves in its magnetism, to imagine it as a metaphor itself for the process of healing, to think through it as much with our hearts as with our minds, and to experience it through the stories and voices of real people who have themselves called upon it as they faced illness.

Poetry defies the restrictive and segregated version of the postmodernist notion of genre, which holds that the form any narrative takes actually molds or shapes experience in order to contain it; unlike a TV miniseries or even a novel, a poem is flexible enough, physically limber enough, to be instead modulated and transformed by the experience it represents, and as such it is exceptionally well disposed to address affliction. Poetry also transcends the limitations of derivative language and, as we have seen, may rather create through more positive constructions opportunities for healing that utilize powers of the imagination science has yet to examine adequately, and which may never be entirely understood; if we accept that negative fantasies about illness can impede healing, then just as surely we can agree that inspiring metaphorical thinking must promote wellness. Certain metaphors (especially modern ones) and narratives (especially postmodern ones) incited by disease may sometimes shield us from the indelicacies of human suffering, or may even fabricate counterfeit representations that enable us to pretend we need not witness it (or can escape it, or have power over it). Yet contemporary poetry about illness, in its particularly embodied use of metaphors and its skintight narrative honesty, stands in contrast as the familiar writhing, panting beast itself—never caged, wildly intelligent, demanding that we listen, and listen, and listen again.

Some readers may say that all that this analysis accomplishes in the end is an idiosyncratic defense, or even a self-serving aggrandizement, of poetry; that instead of distilling essences irrepressibly present in my examples, I have imposed my own biased (and perhaps faulty) narrative upon the same pliable substrate—in short, that my readings conveniently support my own promotion. Other skeptical readers might more generously concede perhaps some small benefit to the ill who write or read poetry, but would quickly add that any sort of "hobby," like gardening or stamp collecting or building airplane models, should just as well provide the same time-occupying, distracting sort of solace. And from others still: *Sure, why not sit them around a table and give them some construction paper and crayons?* I don't have to imagine this dismissive voice; I have actually heard it. *It can't hurt anybody, and maybe they'll keep quiet for a while.*

To these detractors, I would offer from my own clinical practice any of numerous examples of sick people who found in these same poems the kind of sustenance I have tried to describe, and who I believe have lived longer and better lives because of them. I would also point out the increasing interest among respected scientists in the field of mind-body interactions; sponsored by such forward-thinking philanthropies as the Fetzer Institute and the MacArthur Foundation, researchers are beginning to uncover more of the physiological underpinnings of our health responses to cultural phenomena (from large-scale factors such as socioeconomic status to the more intimate realms of sleep and sex behaviors). One of the greatest dividends of a biocultural model of illness with creative self-expression at its center *alongside* scientific inquiry is the enhanced opportunity for collaborations amidst oncologists, say, and those traditionally excluded from investigations of therapeusis, like faith healers and Tibetan monks—or even bona fide literary critics, like my friend Mary Baine Campbell, who wonders whether Milton's famous pair of poems "L'Allegro" and "Il Penseroso" might offer clues as to the neurochemical basis for manic-depressive illness—whereby science does not serve to validate, but rather to help elucidate, and analyses like this one do not simply create impractical beauty but help to ask precise and fruitful questions about empathy. Indeed, it is perhaps my greatest wish to see nonpoet physicians someday use this book with their own patients and medical trainees.

Others might rebuke me for coming down too hard on some too-vague caricature of science—or worse, consign me to the nuttiness of those who indulge their taste for the paranormal or the pietistic. Such reactions, to my mind, are worse than being humored, and more than justify a critique of science as the sole authority on matters of such central importance as those I have taken up here. They seem an expression of precisely the sort of superciliousness that has so often troubled me during my own training in the biomedical model of illness—a model which I have nonetheless readily applauded for all the undiluted relief from suffering it has brought to countless patients. In the end, I hope my interrogation of some of our biomedical "sureties" will provoke not misunderstanding, or resentment, but instead the same kind of dogged, open-minded, even muddy engagement with a question that characterizes the best science, without which we cannot live—and that inspires the best humanistic work, too.

Ontogeny recapitulates phylogeny, I once memorized in medical school; thus I suppose now this book itself enacts what its main thesis is. In writing it, I recognize that I have constructed a kind of narrative, albeit one highly reliant upon poetry, that seeks to make sense of what I observe in my daily work as a physician who is deeply engaged with words. Like the hapless subject of some weird psychology experiment, I am confronted with an instrument (poetry) that I know bears a direct relationship to a process (healing), but which somehow remains separated across a chasm as difficult to conceive of as that which divides the left and right halves of our brains, as stubbornly extant as the old Cartesian mind-body duality. As I wrote this book, this eerie awareness was heightened as I witnessed many of my patients struggling with a similar kind of problem, of reconciling their belief in the basic goodness of people with the profound terror engendered by the events of September 11, 2001; I was struck how, in case after case, resolution seemed to come through storytelling and poem-making. (There is a reason this national trauma is a recurring theme in this book: it represents, terribly and singularly and immediately, the kind of wound to which medicine can never directly minister.) It occurred to me that, like my patients' stories and poems, my book was an effort not just to imagine healing as it strictly relates to illness but to affirm that even the most inadmissible and unconscionable facts

of our existence can yet be visited, wondered at, and narrated—
and thus made human.

Not too long after the terrorist attacks, I traveled to New
York to participate in a reading to help launch a new literary
magazine, the *Bellevue Literary Review*, itself a collaborative effort
between physicians and humanists at New York University and
Bellevue Hospital. While I was there, I visited my dear friend
and mentor Eve Kosofsky Sedgwick. We met for a late lunch at
a soul food restaurant near her apartment in Greenwich Village;
it was also just a few blocks from the St. Vincent Hospital's new
outpatient oncology treatment center, where I learned she was
scheduled for an appointment, something having to do with the
indwelling Portacath hanging limply from her chest, which she
had to fuss with for a moment over our crispy fried chicken and
steaming grits. Eve is perhaps best known for her peerless liter-
ary scholarship; she is the founder of a controversial academic
discipline, postmodern in its bent, known as "queer theory." She
has also written brilliantly and valuably of her experience of
breast cancer, and the depression that followed the diagnosis. As
we walked the few long blocks to the treatment center, the city
streets unusually free of traffic, quiet enough that I noticed the
skittering of trash across them and the buffeting of the chill
wind, I looked into the drawn faces of the passersby.

Eve had been recounting the special kindness New Yorkers
had been showing to one another in the days since the tragedy; I
remembered, as I searched the expressions of strangers, the wall
of photographs of the missing that lined the passageway to Belle-
vue's main entrance, the hammed-up smiles and feigned looks of

surprise—fragments of private stories between the dead and their loved ones—that had brought tears to my eyes. Seamlessly, the topic of our conversation shifted; Eve was going on to talk about her newest project, writing an advice column for *MAMM*, a smart new magazine for breast cancer survivors, and her special excitement about helping to create a film about women living with metastatic disease. Five years ago, she learned that the neck pain she had been having for months—I'd once spent a whole harrowing afternoon on hold with her, the telephone receiver droning a tinny Beethoven sonata, as she tried to get medical attention for it from her HMO—was the result of the spread of cancer to her cervical spine. She was not supposed to be alive now, according to the strictly biomedical narrative of my oncology textbooks; at the end of my indoctrinating residency training back then, I had been as pessimistic as her own physicians about the prospects for long-term survival, wondering grimly whether she might be a candidate for bone marrow transplantation, or at the very least, more chemotherapy.

Among the many responses Eve had to her poor prognosis, one was to write a book, one that was very different from any of the more dense scholarly tomes she had previously conceived. Entitled *A Dialogue on Love*, it explores through haibun (a fascinating Japanese verse form that combines lyrical prose and delicate haiku), interleaved with excerpts from her therapist's otherwise unedited notes, her treatment for the recurrence and the concomitant depression she also suffered, charting how she endured. Walking beside her arm in arm, feeling the warmth of her body against mine, I knew her poetry was as much a reason for her survival as were whatever drugs she was having infused through her Portacath; we embraced, and she turned to smile at me when she reached the top of the stairs, before disappearing into the monolithic clinic's shiny revolving door. As I stood on the sidewalk feeling her absence, I was reminded of a passage from her book, near the end, when she has come to terms with the possibility of her mortality, which leaves her not more depressed but rather with a sense of peace and joy. It seems fitting to close with an excerpt from her book, indeed a dialogue between her mental health provider's notes (in small caps) and her own wise words, which together say as much about empathy as they do about endings:

TESTS SHOW NO NEW CANCER; TESTS SHOW SAME OLD CANCER. SPINAL PAIN REMAINS BUT SOME LESS. E WORKING ON HOW TO LIVE IN RELATION TO AN INCURABLE, NOT PRESENTLY DEBILITATING, ILLNESS. TALKING ABOUT THE NUMBER OF PEOPLE WHO ASK IF THE NEWS IS GOOD OR BAD—THAT IS NOT A FLEXIBLE OR PRODUCTIVE WAY OF THINKING ABOUT THIS. AN AIM NOT TO HOPE OR FEAR A LOT, NOT LEAD OTHERS TO.

———

Here's a Buddhist meditation I've read about. I can even do it.

It happens in a public place; the substance of it is to recognize that every other person there, one by one, male and female and young and old, has been, in some earlier life, your mother.

Or more likely, in many lives.

And regarding the people one by one, you learn to understand how this could have been so. One by one as you gaze, you can see what kind of mother they were to you; you can see as well, slowly, slowly, what kind of child you were to them.

Over and over

you're like Aeneas
encountering a stranger,
Venus, and guessing,

just from the rosy
glow of their neck and their feet,
and their stately step,

though too late, "Surely,
stranger, you are a goddess.
Surely, my mother."

Shy as I am, I'm pretty good at this meditation.

In almost every face I can find the curve of a tenderness, however hidden. The place of a smile, or an intelligence—a shared one.

Aeneas: "Why am I never allowed to take your hand in mine, to hear your true voice and speak to you as you really are?"

Even in a skinhead without any lips to speak of; or

in a girl who's anxious, anorexic, half crazed with all her narcissistic burden—even from her I can elicit and nurture it, the sense of her possible, beautiful care of me. Indeed, of a compassion; of her imagination, or his.

The contrast between Eve's words and her therapist's is a telling one. One utters a clinical litany of fact and detachment, attentively, even with care, but (necessarily) from without; the other unabashedly declaims a poetry of myth, and empathy, words much more directly shaped by the illness experience as it is *lived*. Ironically, it is the dialogue between these two deep modes of understanding—the dialogue that Eve so rightly names as pertaining to love—that leads to her healing, both emotionally and physically. She joins, across the incomplete rupture of the semicolon, "compassion" and "imagination." The secret of Eve's survival, as she records it, seems to be this ability to discern love, to extract it, through the kind of acutely open consciousness that poetry arouses, and then rejoins to those around it, from which each of us too long has remained estranged—to share, again and again, in the unknowable and yet unmistakable touch of the divine.

Further Reading

So far-reaching is the connection between poetry and healing that many other important works by a diverse group of writers—largely poets, but also scientists, philosophers, playwrights, novelists, and memoirists—might well have amplified this book. Because of space considerations and a primary devotion to poetry, I had to make difficult choices about what ultimately to leave out. What follows is an informal catalogue of some of these other invaluable writings. Because even this bibliography must be limited, I will include here only works by essentially contemporary and mostly American authors—one attempting to list all relevant sources (from Sophocles' cathartic drama *Oedipus Rex* to the healing chants of medieval abbess Hildegard von Bingen to Tolstoy's and Mann's transforming life-and-death narratives *The Death of Ivan Ilyich* and *The Magic Mountain*) would surely be as long as another book, if not several!

To begin with poetry, perhaps the work of Jane Kenyon, who died of leukemia in 1995, is the most sorely lacking in my discussion. Her final book, *Otherwise: New and Collected Poems*, published posthumously in 1996 by Graywolf Press, is a stunning document of the human will to survive, and is one I think anyone confronting illness should read, and reread. Her husband Donald Hall's books *Without* (Houghton Mifflin, 1998) and *The Painted Bed* (Houghton Mifflin, 2002) are as much about grief as they are enactments of the soul's repair. If Kenyon's and Hall's work, taken together, is ultimately about restoring through poetry a particularly sweet life lost to the world, then blind poet Steven Kuusisto's book *Only Bread Only Light* (Copper Canyon Press, 2000) accomplishes the same for sight, in words that gleam in the mind's eye. Sharon Olds, whose incomparable poems are a triumph of beauty and sensuality, and in some sense forgiveness, over the harm caused by parental physical and psychological abuse (*Satan Says*, University of Pittsburgh Press, 1985; *The Father*, Random House, 1992; as well as much of her more recent work), besides all that she has given us on the page, also teaches a writing workshop at a psychiatric hospital in New York. Elizabeth Arnold's *The Reef* (University of Chicago Press, 1999) explores the experience of breast cancer as though her own body were a gorgeous, submerged wreck, locus of both loss and resurgent life at once. Abba Kovner's *Sloan Kettering: Poems* (Schocken Books, 2002) is a Holocaust survivor's harrowing and yet heroic poetic meditation on revisiting the prospect of death, only narrowly escaped so many decades before. Elizabeth Hall Hutner's *Life with Sam* (CavanKerry Press, 2002) breathes life back into the poet's young son, whose untimely death from leukemia is thus transformed into a celebration of love and a declaration of survival. Lucille Clifton, National Book Award winner for *Blessing the Boats: New and Selected Poems* (BOA Editions, 2000), makes her own afflicted body, ravaged by kidney failure and cancer, the subject of numerous poems throughout her long and distinguished career, which seem to function at once as transcendent spirituals and her own brand of down-to-earth body-music. Alan Shapiro, in *The Dead Alive and Busy* (University of Chicago Press, 1998) and *Song and Dance* (Houghton Mifflin, 2002), gives us poetry infused with the pain of inconceivable loss as he cares for first his sister and then his brother, each one dying slowly and painfully of cancer; not just stirring elegies, these poems provide eloquent proof of empathy's invincible power to sustain us even in the face of death's cruelest acts.

A few disease entities in particular have spawned more than a handful of other noteworthy collections of verse. Poets Marie Howe (*What the Living Do*, W. W. Norton, 1999) and Richard McCann (*Ghost Letters*, Alice James Books, 1994) both make indelible contributions to the poetry of healing in their responses to the AIDS pandemic, refusing any distinction between bearing witness to suffering and suffering itself; David Bergman (*Heroic Measures*, Ohio State University Press, 1998) and Michael Klein (*1990*, Provincetown Arts Press, 1993) similarly address AIDS with unflinching honesty and unfailing grace. Hilda Raz (*Divine Honors*, Wesleyan University Press, 1997) and Judith Hall (*Anatomy, Errata*, Ohio State University Press, 1998), in their courageous writing about breast cancer, invent a kind of cure through their masterful deployment of language; Debra Bruce, another breast cancer survivor, also overcomes infertility in a sequence of sonnets that forms the heart of her collection *What Wind Will Do* (Miami University Press, 1997). Sherod Santos (*The Pilot Star Elegies*, W. W. Norton, 1999) and Nick Flynn (*Some Ether*, Graywolf Press, 2000) forge poems strong enough to contain all the conflicting emotions they feel in the wake of that most unfathomable of wounds to the self—suicide—which robs each of a close family member.

Still others who have written significantly about other health conditions as varied as aging and Alzheimer's disease, addiction and alcoholism, arthritis and depression and lung disease (in numerous individual poems that are beyond the scope of my annotations here), include such greats as Hayden Carruth, Rachel Hadas, Edward Hirsch, Richard Howard, Stanley Kunitz, Sylvia Plath, Stanley Plumly, Adrienne Rich, Anne Sexton, and May Swenson. The likes of Yehuda Amichai, Mahmud Darwish, Martín Espada, June Jordan, Marge Piercy, Muriel Rukeyser, Peter Dale Scott, and Adam Zagajewski deserve mention also for their generous poetry (perhaps for some in part inspired by personal encounters with illness) that seeks to cure our broken society of its cynicism and enmity. The wide-ranging poetry of care providers, put forth by nurses and doctors alike, has been especially important to me in my own chimerical existence; it is too numerous a roster to mention by name, but I direct the reader to the anthologies of their work *Between the Heartbeats: Poetry and Prose by Nurses* and *Blood and Bones: Poems by Physicians* (University of Iowa Press, 1995 and 1998, respectively) to feel their therapeutic laying on of hands evoked in languages.

Lastly, I must call the reader's attention to the many anthologies of poetry that respond to illness, in the pages of which one finds represented these and nearly every important poet of our times, as if to underscore the utter inescapability of this intersection between art, body, and science: *Articulations: The Body and Illness in Poetry* (University of Iowa Press, 1994), *Poets for Life: 76 Poets Respond to the AIDS Epidemic* (Persea Books, 1982), and *Beyond Bedlam: Poems Written out of Mental Distress* (Dufour Editions, 1998) are all good places to start; of equal interest in this regard are the anthologies that collect the poetry of writers newly born in their experiences of illness, such as *The Cancer Poetry Project: Poems by Cancer Patients and Those Who Love Them* (Fairview Press, 2001) and *Unending Dialogue: Voices from an AIDS Poetry Workshop* (Faber and Faber, 1993). Without the heartening work of all of these fine poets, my own work as a physician and poet would have been impossible, as would have been the writing of this book.

In the realm of prose, the poets who have crossed into this genre have instructed me the most meaningfully, with the following books: Paul Monette's *Becoming a Man: Half a Life Story* (Harper San Francisco, 1993), winner of the National Book Award, perhaps the most important examination of AIDS in America; Audre Lorde's *The Cancer Journals* (Aunt Lute Books, 1980), which like Monette's memoir pits the power of the particular, personal imagination against the unfeeling machine of biomedicine; William Carlos Williams's *Autobiography* (W. W. Norton, 1967), an astonishing account of a life in which healing and language merged, sometimes tensely, but always productively; Alan Shapiro's *Vigil* (University of Chicago Press, 1997), which probes with a sensitivity equal to his poems the limits of grief, and returns scarred but also renewed; and Stephen Kuusisto's *The Planet of the Blind* (Delta, 1998), which speaks directly to how the pursuit of poetry brings some light into the darkness of visual loss.

Other poets' memoirs further expand on the theme of language as a healing modality. Sandra Gilbert's *Wrongful Death: A Medical Tragedy* (W. W. Norton, 1995) provides a searing critique of the biomedical model's inability to hear the patient's voice, and the terrible consequences of her husband's death from such negligence, all the while refusing to yield the poet's lyricism. In *Autobiography of a Face* (Houghton Mifflin, 1994), Lucy Grealy similarly finds solace in poetry, as a rare bone cancer and the aggressive treatment brought to bear upon it disfigures her. Suzanne Berger's *Horizontal Woman: The Story of a Body in Exile* (Houghton Mifflin, 1996) demonstrates how language can stand upright even when the author, debilitated by undiagnosable lower back pain, cannot. Yet another notable memoir of illness experience that lends further support to the notion that language can heal is the great novelist and poet Reynolds Price's *A Whole New Life* (Atheneum, 1994), which chronicles the central role of storytelling and spirituality in his recovery from a deadly spinal cord cancer, and in surmounting his resultant disability.

Not only poets have testified to the necessity of language in contending with illness. Beloved literary critic Anatole Broyard's *Intoxicated by My Illness and Other Writings on Life and Death* (Fawcett, 1998) is further required reading, for its especially self-conscious account of the use of literature in coming to terms with his disease, prostate cancer. Nancy Mairs, the author of *Waist-High in the World: Life Among the Nondisabled* and *The Troubled Guest: Life and Death Stories* (Beacon Press, 1998 and 2002, respectively), reflects in supple, moving language upon disability (in her case, brought on by multiple sclerosis) and the access it paradoxically affords to the too-little-trafficked imaginative and spiritual realms of our lives, and even to the acceptance of mortality. Other remarkable (and widely popular) memoirs of illness in which language figures as a crucial therapeutic instrument have been written by Mitch Albom (*Tuesdays with Morrie*, Doubleday, 1997), Susanna Kaysen (*Girl, Interrupted*, Vintage Books, 1994), William Styron (*Darkness Visible: A Memoir of Madness*, Vintage Books, 1992), Ben Watt (*Patient*, Grove Press, 1998), and another quite recent National Book Award winner, Andrew Solomon (*The Noonday Demon: An Atlas of Depression*, Scribner, 2001). Anne Fadiman's *The Spirit Catches You and You Fall Down: A Hmong Child, Her American Doctors, and the Collision of Two Cultures* (Farrar, Straus and Giroux, 1997) and Michael Bérubé's *Life as We Know It: A Father, a Family, and an Exceptional Child* (Random House, 1996) are riveting accounts of affliction as observed in the strictest sense from without—their authors do not suffer themselves from epilepsy or Down's syndrome—and yet well demonstrate how we as community and family participate in illness by sharing through words its difficult teachings with others. Beth Kephart's *A Slant of Sun: One Child's Courage* (W. W. Norton, 1998), the unsentimental account of her son's struggle with "pervasive developmental disorder, not otherwise specified," and Jamaica Kincaid's bracing *My Brother* (Farrar, Straus, and Giroux, 1997), in which AIDS causes a troubled brother and a world-weary sister to resume (and in some sense, to rescue) their relationship, also belong in this fine company. Among more academic writers, Arthur Frank's scholarship in this area is to me equal in importance to that of Sontag and Morris. His two brilliant books, *At the Will of the Body: Reflections on Illness* (Houghton Mifflin, 1991) and *The Wounded Storyteller: Body, Illness, and Ethics* (University of Chicago Press, 1995), draw on his own experience of testicular cancer and his training as a sociologist to formulate, primarily, an elegant argument for the indispensability of personal narratives in determining both diagnostic and therapeutic approaches to disease. Elaine Scarry's classic treatise on pain, *The Body in Pain* (Oxford University Press, 1985), is another humane explication of a biological phenomenon that is at the same time a complex social construct. Medievalist and poet Mary B. Campbell's *Wonder and Science: Imagining Worlds in Early Modern Europe* (Cornell University Press, 1999) is a thrilling journey back to a time when the territories of literary writing (especially poetry and travel writing) and science overlapped, and when the "anthropological" practice of each informed the other in startling ways. In a related vein, philosopher Mary Midgley gives us *Poetry and Science* (Routledge, 2001), which proposes a kind a reconciliation between the arts and the sciences, based on a clear-eyed debunking of some of the popular fallacies about their genesis that have in recent times so torn them asunder; *Muddling Through: The Pursuit of Science and Truths in the 21st Century*

Further Reading

(Counterpoint Press, 1998), collaboratively written by scientist Herbert Bernstein and humanist Michael Fortun, by exposing the real-life subjective messiness of scientific inquiry, similarly refutes misconscptions of science as a purely objective and always unerring pursuit of fact. Poetry therapist John Fox's *Poetic Medicine: The Healing Art of Poem-making* (J. P. Tarcher, 1997) and Louise DeSalvo's *Writing as a Way of Healing: How Telling Our Stories Transforms Our Lives* (Beacon Press, 2000) are at once moving manifestos for the use of poetry in specific clinical applications and also intelligent, practical guides for how to do so. I am also grateful to such humanist scientists as Lewis Thomas (himself a physician) and Stephen Jay Gould for exemplifying how the most rigorous science is always best understood as an expression of creative and sometimes quirky human minds.

One unique resource for all who wish to investigate further the arts and medicine is New York University's medical humanities web site, Literature, Arts and Medicine, which can be found at http://endeavor.med.nyu.edu/lit-med/. Curated by Dr. Felice Aull, an accomplished poet and scientist, it is a clearinghouse of information about many of the writers I have discussed in this book and detailed annotations on their work, and on many others who may have written more occasionally or incidentally about illness. Additional information on visual artists who have represented illness in their work, as well as a compendium of medical school curricula in the medical humanities, may also be found there. Two scholarly journals, *Literature and Medicine* and the *Journal of the Medical Humanities*, edited respectively by the well-known medical humanists Rita Charon and Delese Wear, publish research relating to medical historiography and narrative ethics, reviews of literary works dealing with the illness experience, and other cogent academic work. A handful of the most prestigious academic medical journals, such as *JAMA* and the *Annals of Internal Medicine,* regularly present poetry arising from encounters with medicine.

I will conclude by pointing out two acclaimed playwrights whose work epitomizes the timeless drama of the relationship between the arts, the body, and illness. Tony Kushner reinvented (and revived) American theater by drawing it back to its ancient roots in the classical cathartic *tragedia* while addressing the entirely new disease AIDS with *Angels in America* and *Perestroika.* On a smaller scale, Margaret Edson's near-perfect play *Wit*— about an English professor who specializes in Donne's metaphysical sonnets facing brute death from ovarian cancer—left me speechless when I first saw it; I know of no other work that so fiercely makes plain that in poetry, that purest idiom of our hearts, that sacred text inscribed by our bodies upon the unthinking world, reside the keys to the mystery of healing.

Permissions